WRITE ON

The Kid-Friendly Mother-Pleasing Gentle Way To Learn to Write

By Karen K. Newell

SECOND EDITION
ISBN 9780975499788

With thanks to the children whose writing has been included in this curriculum:

Matthew,
Karalee,
Bradford,
Caleb

1st Edition 2003
2nd Edition 2012

ISBN 9780975499788

Published by Learn For Your Life, 308 Prowell Drive, Camp Hill, PA 17011

If you have feedback, questions or suggestions concerning Write On please contact us at *www.kid-friendly-homeschool-curriculum.com*.

Dedication

In Memory of my father,
Alfred F. Bobbitt

And Honor of my mother,
Donna Lee Bobbitt

TABLE OF CONTENTS

(➊ Introduces the next Write On)

(Bolded—Progressive Structured Reports)

WRITE ON

Put away your red marking pen, roll up your sleeves, and get ready to become a writing coach. This book is not about assigning and grading students' writing. It is about getting students and parents interacting with writing.

Before going further, take a moment to look at how the writing pages are laid out. Each page is called a Write On and has its own number. The title of each Write On and its corresponding number can be found in the upper right hand corner.

The most prominent feature of each Write On is the sample writing done by a student. Before beginning the writing process, sit down and read the writing sample with your young writer. The writing samples are non-intimidating so your student can feel, "I can do *that.*"

On top of the page, in the center, is the objective box. This lets the student and parent know the purpose of the Write On. In some cases, it will state that this is an introduction to the next Write On. In these cases, the student's written work for this first Write On will become the basis for the next. It also indicates to the writing coach that both should be done before proceeding to the next writing level. The writing levels are described in detail on the next pages.

You will also notice there is a direction box, shaped like an arrow, in the upper left hand corner. This gives the writing coach the steps to proceed through the writing process.

Finally, at the bottom of the page, you may see one or more idea clouds. These may include optional ideas, alternatives, or writing starters.

The table of contents lists the 100 Write On lessons. You will notice that some of the Write On lessons are bolded in the table of contents. These are the Progressive Structured Reports that gradually lead the student from writing sentences, to paragraphs, to essays, then compositions, and finally preparing a thesis.

Notice I said "gradually." One can do the math and realize that if a student did one Write On per day, it would take three and a half months to complete the book. But it is not realistic to think that in less than four months a third or fourth grader will be writing a thesis.

Instead, the progression one will see over several months will not be numerically, from one end of the book to the next. The progression will be in depth, as the student progresses through the four levels of writing for each Write On.

WHAT WE WISH TO AVOID

Before discussing the writing in each level, let's examine what we don't want our students to do. Consider these scenarios:

> After being told to write a one page paper describing a recent field trip, Alicia is sitting at the table staring out the window chewing on her pencil. There is nothing on her paper.
>
> Nick has been given an assignment to write a two to three page paper on one of the founding fathers. After several days, he turns in a 1 ½ page paper with large writing. It is obvious he was trying to make it seem like he has written more. There is no organization to the content.

Samantha has been told to write a paragraph using descriptive writing. Her paragraph has very little descriptive language.

In these scenarios, the students are told to do an assignment, but don't have the skills to do them. It would be like handing a beginning piano student a complex piece of music and expecting him to sit down and play it.

In contrast, students can be taught writing skills by having someone coach them on how to apply their own ideas to the written page. To do that, we need to differentiate between Learning to Write (the first three levels) and Writing to Learn (the fourth level.)

LEARNING TO WRITE or WRITING TO LEARN

How does a student learn to write, play the piano, ride a bike, do a math problem, cook a holiday meal, or any other skill? He or she needs to be shown how to do it, and given the opportunity to practice. The skill level will increase with practice.

With Write On, the student is shown a writing skill, and given three opportunities to practice it. With each practice level, the amount of independence and complexity increases. This is what is meant by Learning to Write.

When a student is Writing to Learn, she uses a skill she has already mastered to explore content in another subject area. She can concentrate on the content, confident in her ability to use the writing skills she has already learned and practiced.

For example, when a student is first introduced to the concept of writing a paragraph, he will write paragraphs about things he is familiar with. His concentration and focus is on this new skill of developing paragraphs.

If the student is introduced to the concept of paragraphs and expected to write a paragraph on a subject that is he is now just learning – for example, the atomic theory - he has two new areas of focus and can be overwhelmed.

First, he learns to write paragraphs, and once he has advanced through to the level of mastery, he can write a paragraph about atomic theory, concentrating his efforts on understanding and explaining these new scientific ideas.

In the first three levels, then, students are learning to write. In the fourth level, they are writing to learn. The process can be summed up in this table.

Learning to Write

	Level	Parents' Role	Usual Subject Matter
Level One	Beginner	Writes with student	Familiar to the student
Level Two	Intermediate	Gives prompts, cues	Common
Level Three	Advanced	Suggests improvements	Less Common

Writing to Learn

	Level	Parent's Role	Usual Subject Matter
Level Four	Mastery	Supports ideas	Academic

LEVEL ONE WORKING TOGETHER

The first time a student does a Write On, she will do it at Level One – Writing Together. The writing coach looks at the Write On with the student and together they read and discuss the sample writing. The student chooses a topic she would like to write about. It is usually most effective if she chooses something familiar and interesting to her. This is particularly important if the writing skill is new or challenging for her.

The student and coach can then discuss how the topic can be approached. Through the entire assignment, the student and coach are working together.

As an example, let's listen as one coach/student team develops a written report for Write On #15. For our purposes here, it may help if you examine Write On 15 and Write On 16 (which builds on 15) to better understand this process.

Sample Dialogue: Level One

Coach: Now that we have read this sample, it's time for you to do one. Is there an animal you would like to write a Three Sentence Report on?

Student: I want to write about my rabbit.

(Notice he chose something familiar. If he were to choose an animal he knows very little about, it may be better to guide him to something familiar at this level.)

Coach: A rabbit is a good choice. What three things can you tell me about rabbits?

Student: They are furry.

Coach: Good point. What should we write, "Rabbits are.....?"

Student: Rabbits are covered with fur.

(The first sentence is written down.)

Coach: Okay, what else can you write about rabbits?

Student: They eat plants.

Coach: That's important as well. How should we write that?

Student: Rabbits are plant eaters.

(This is also written down.)

Coach: You have a good start on your report. Now we need only one more.

Student: Rabbits are soft.

(The coach realizes that soft and furry are closely connected and it will be difficult to develop two distinct paragraphs for Write On 16. Therefore, the student will be guided away from this point.)

Coach: Soft is related to the rabbits' fur which you already described. Can you tell me something completely different about them?

Student: They have long ears.

Coach: Why do they have long ears?

Student: Because they need good hearing to get away from their enemies.

Coach: You have a choice here. You could write about their ears, and say something like, "Rabbits have long ears" or you could tell about their hearing and say something like, "Rabbits need sharp hearing to survive."

Student: I'd like to write about their hearing.

Step by step, the student and coach are interacting with the material. The student is succeeding in applying his ideas to the written structure without struggling to understand what is expected of him. At this level, it is even acceptable for the coach to do the actual physical work of writing down the sentences the student develops orally. When the coach does the writing by the student's dictation, however, the student may benefit from copying the sentences in his own handwriting. Regardless of how the physical writing is done, the student should be affirmed for developing his own ideas and sentences.

LEVEL TWO
USING PROMPTS AND CUES

After creating a written work with the coach, and being affirmed for successfully writing about their chosen topic, the student will have more confidence in his or her ability to do the writing presented in that Write On. In the second level, the coach discusses the ideas with the student before the actual writing is done. The coach may give prompts. She may write down on a card some of the ideas discussed as a cues for the student to use. It may help to write down the spelling of words that may be unfamiliar.

When two Write On lessons are paired together, the first one will state in the objective box that it is an introduction to the second. For instance, Write On 15 is an introduction to Write On 16. In these situations, the student will do both lessons at the first level before proceeding to the second level with the earlier assignment. In our example, the student completed Write On 16 and developed her three sentences into three paragraphs about rabbits with the coach's guidance. Now she is going to tackle Write On 15 again, but this time at Level Two.

Sample Dialogue for Level Two

Coach: You did a great job doing the Three Sentence Report about rabbits. Let's choose another animal, and you will write a different report. Is there an animal you are interested in?

Student: Alligators

Coach: Okay, alligators would make a fun report to read about. What can you tell me about them?

Student: They live in swamps.

Coach: Fine, I'll write "swamp" on this card. What else?

Student: They are reptiles.

Coach: I'll write "reptiles" here as well. What else?

Student: I can't think of anything else.

Coach: You've told me what kind of animal they are and where they live. Can you tell me about their diet, or how they produce young, or about their personalities?

Student: They eat swamp animals and fish.

Coach: That's true. Do you want to say they are carnivores or that they eat animals?

At this level the coach is giving prompts before the writing begins. If she finds the student is getting bogged down during the writing process, she may intervene with suggestions to help get a sentence started.

LEVEL THREE
WRITING WITH INDEPENDENCE

At the third level, the student demonstrates greater independence. The coach discusses his ideas with him but doesn't write the words down for the report. She may encourage him to write down his ideas in outline form during their pre-writing discussion.

Sample Dialogue

Coach: You wrote two reports on animals: rabbits and alligators. You are going to finish this project by writing a third report on a different animal. Do you have any ideas?

Student: How about fish?

Coach: Let's be more specific. Is there a particular fish you can tell others about?

Student: Maybe sword fish.

Coach: That's a good idea and would make an interesting report. Would you like to tell me your ideas, or would you rather work on it alone?

If the student has difficulty coming up with ideas, the coach can ask them questions to draw ideas out of them.

LEVEL FOUR
MASTERY

At this point, the student has written three reports using the same writing skills. He should have developed a comfort level with this skill. Now, instead of Learning to Write with this skill, he can use it in order to Write to Learn.

Sample Dialogue Level Four

Coach: Remember when you did the Three Sentence Report about animals? You are going to use that for your science unit study. Today I want you to read your book about planets, and write a Three Sentence Report about any of the planets.

The writing coach should keep a list of all the Write On lessons the student has successfully achieved independence and mastery. This list can be consulted when assigning written work for the student's writing for other subjects.

QUESTIONS ABOUT WRITE ON

Does the student have to do all four levels with each Write On?

No. Some students may demonstrate sufficient skill after doing it only one time. In this case, you may want to put it in your list of Write On lessons that have been mastered.

On the other hand, some students may be more challenged by a particular skill, or by writing in general. There is nothing magical about the number four. It may take seven or eight times for them to achieve the level of mastery. With the student who struggles with the writing process, it is even more important to focus on writing about topics of their interest and affirming small successes.

How long should it take to complete all one hundred Write On lessons?

The length of time depends on the student's writing ability and his or her proficiency of writing when the course is begun. The goal is to develop writing proficiency over a course of several years, not in one or two written assignments.

How are the Progressive Structured Reports different from the other Write On lessons?

All the bolded Write On lessons in the table of contents are Progressive Structured Reports (PSR's). This is academic writing that is structured and progresses in difficulty to the writing of paragraphs, essays, longer compositions, and finally a thesis. Again, you should not expect that many students can progress to writing a thesis the same year they learn how to construct a paragraph. The student should have multiple opportunities to succeed at each skill before proceeding to the next PSR.

Do we start at Write On 1?

It is not necessary to start at the beginning. Look at the Progressive Structured Reports (those divisible by five) and determine your student's current writing skill. For some students, it may be helpful to give a review by starting at the skill level one step easier than their current skill. But certainly a student who has been writing essays does not need to start with the construction of sentences, unless that is an area of weakness that should be reviewed.

How much attention should be given to the creative writing skills between the Progressive Structured Reports?
The amount of attention you give to the lessons that focus on creative skills will depend on your student. There are two different types of students that often enjoy the creative writing more than others. One is the natural writer. This is the student with a natural writing ability who enjoys using a variety of styles. These students often enjoy playing with words and phrases and are quite creative in their writing.

Another student who may enjoy the creative writing comes from the other end of the writing spectrum. The reluctant writer who dreads holding a pencil long enough to construct a paragraph may enjoy the success of these lessons, which are usually shorter and more entertaining. One goal of a creative Write On is to give such students a taste of success and take away the aversion to writing.

We should mention that there is another young writer who may not appreciate the creative lessons. This is the down to earth, pragmatic student who wants no bells and whistles. "Give me my work and let me do it and be done with it," may be his approach to his studies and such writing may seem unnecessary and even foolish to him.
Each writing coach should evaluate the needs, interests, and skills of their students when choosing how to incorporate Write On into the students' studies.

PUTTING IT ALL TOGETHER

Obviously, no two students are going to progress through Write On at the same pace. While each student is different, it may help to give a general guideline on how to proceed.

Assuming that the student is doing the Progressive Structured Reports at his or her current writing ability, it may take six to eight weeks to progress to the next PSR. At the risk of sounding like a broken record, it should be emphasized that some will progress this far in a week or two, and others may take much longer.

Start by looking ahead for the next five Write On lessons. Which of these may take longer?

You may find it helpful to do the PSR one time at the first level. Then, before proceeding to the second level, the student may enjoy being introduced to one of the creative Write On lessons in between. It may be easiest for the writing coach to do these lessons in the order they come in, just to keep track of where they are in the program. But that certainly is not necessary, and one may find it beneficial to pick and choose the order.

After doing the creative writing, the student may return and do the PSR at the second level. In this case, the student would do each of the creative lessons between the PSR, and by the time he has reached the level of mastery, he is ready to progress to the next set of five lessons. That may look like this:

PSR Write On 10 – Level One
Write On 11
PSR Write On 10 – Level Two
Write On 12
PSR Write On 10 - Level Three
Write On 13
PSR Write On 10 – Level Four
Write On 14

Also, it is possible for the student to do the shorter, creative lessons through the four levels as well. In many cases, it may be redundant to do it four times, but again the coach will assess the ability of that Write On to meet the needs of the student.

Keep in mind that during this period of time the student will not only be Learning to Write, but also Writing to Learn. The more unfamiliar the material he is writing about for his other subjects of study, the easier the Write On skill that should be chosen. There is no need to stay within the five Write On lessons for his Writing to Learn assignments. Instead, feel free to go back to any Write On that gives the student tools for reporting in written form what he is studying.

EVALUATING YOUR STUDENTS WRITING

Evaluating and grading students' written work is part of the learning process. The writing coach should focus the evaluation on rewarding strengths and improving areas of weakness.

Below is a simple but efficient way to grade writing. Choose ten criteria that will be used to evaluate the writing. For each criteria, the student can achieve up to ten points.

Some of the criteria you may wish to use for grading are listed here. Any ten that are most applicable to the lesson can be chosen. It may be helpful to the student if a grading criteria sheet is devised before she begins writing. That gives the student the opportunity of knowing what she should focus on. In this case, the grading criteria becomes part of the learning process.

Content

Ideas communicated clearly
Explanations are logical
Originality of ideas
Gets the readers attention
Paragraph development
Outline is well organized
Introduction
Conclusion
Bibliography
Neatness of paper
Art work
Directions were followed
Paper completed on time
Accomplishes the stated purpose (state what the purpose is)
Improvement in area of previous weakness (state what that area is)

Mechanics

Spelling
Grammar
Punctuation

There is a simple strategy for grading the criteria for the students' content. If it is clear that the student has put forth effort in developing her paper and satisfactorily done the lesson, you may want to give nine out of ten points as the basic grade for each criteria. If there is something specific for any criteria that is stronger, give ten points and tell the student what she did that was exceptional. For any weak areas, deduct one point, or in some cases two or more points, and again give a specific explanation.

If it is apparent that the students' effort is lacking, eight points for each criteria may be more appropriate. With nine points, the average grade would be a 90%, which is a reasonable grade for a good paper with a grade of B, and gives a starting point for him to earn the additional points towards an A. If an eight point scale is used as the basic grade, an average of 80% is indicated. The coach can use whatever base points that are appropriate, as long as the reasoning is consistent.

Grading the mechanics is a little more objective, but the basic standard will be dependent on the writing coach. To begin with, consider deducting one point per paragraph per error. For instance, if the student wrote five paragraphs and has ten spelling errors, then two points out of ten is deducted.

Mechanics should count if the paper was assigned and several days given to write it, because the student had time to improve the mechanics after the content was produced. For writing that is done in one sitting and handed in, mechanics should not be emphasized, and primarily the content evaluated. In other words, the mechanics can account for 50% of the grade, or 0% of the grade, or anywhere in between.

Just as the athletic coach is not the judge for an athlete's competitive performance, some writing coaches do not grade the final report. You may want to consider having another parent, teacher, or other individual do the grading. The writing coach should still select the criteria by which the paper is graded.

TIPS FROM THE TRENCHES

Each family will develop their own way of incorporating Write On into their educational program. Here are some ideas that have been used:

Keep a file folder for each number of Write On, and put all the written assignments a student completes for that Write On in the correct folder.

The student may choose one of their written works for each Write On as the one they wish to submit for a grade. Those assignments go through the complete proofing and editing process.

Use art work, stickers, colored stationary for the printer, or scrap booking supplies to give selected written works a flare.

While going through the Learning to Write process, the teacher assigns the Write On for the student to do. When the student uses the Writing to Learn process to report on information they are learning in a unit study, the student chooses which Write On they wish to develop.

Some students find correcting the mechanics to be drudgery, and dread the writing process because of it. It helps to separate the writing from the editing process. In your writing lessons, focus entirely on the development of content. Later, use their unedited writings as the basis for grammar lessons.

Students often appreciate clues as they do the detective work of finding their mechanical errors (or "crimes".) Give them a list of things to find. For example:

- spelling errors - 3
- run on sentences – 2
- omitted apostrophe – 2
- incorrect homonyms – 1

The student needs to read the writing one time while hunting for each type of error.

FINALLY

As parents, we watch our children grow as they learn to walk, and talk, and read, and numerous other skills. Writing is one of the more complex tasks your child will learn, and as such it is a slow process. Enjoy the process with them. Encourage their ideas and guide their use of proper mechanics. At the end of each year you both will be rewarded with a portfolio of their writing progress.

Write On #1
PICTURE WORDS

Objectives

1. *Word play*
2. *Use adjectives*
3. *Introduce Write On #2*

DIRECTIONS

1. Think of an adjective.
An adjective could fit in this blank:
The ________ puppy.

2. Write your word in letters that show the word's trait.

Rising

Thin

Make a poster of your picture words.
Let everyone contribute.

Write your words on an index card and put them in a box where no one sees them. At the end of the week someone can read the words.

Let everyone make a picture from the cards that are read. See who gets closest to the original.

Objective
Creative writing

DIRECTIONS

1. Use your picture cards to write a picture story.

2. Use a colored marker if you have any color words.

Your picture words can make a picture story.

One morning a little boy was 

rounded red ball. It was not easy to bounce the ball and walk on the crooked road at the same time. The little boy tripped on the cracked pavement. As he fell he saw a fat wiggly worm on the sidewalk. When the hairy worm looked up, he saw the falling boy coming right towards him. The worm curled up into a tiny ball. “Hmm,” said the boy after he landed, “I wonder if I can 

Write On #3
ACRONYMS

Objectives
1. Report information
2. Organize content

DIRECTIONS

1. Make a list about the important qualities about a person or object.

2. Determine how many letters are in the word. This is the number of facts you will report. Some of your facts may need to be deleted of combined.

3. Write the word vertically with one letter on each line.

4. Match letters in the word with the facts you have listed.

5. If you have difficulty, see the help page on the back of this sheet.

Acronyms can report a lot of information with a few words.

A*n honest man*
B*orn in Kentucky*
R*econciliation with the South*
A *tall bearded man*
H*ated Slavery*
A *home schooled child*
M*an who become our 16th president*

L*oving to others*
I*ntelligen*t
N*ortherner*
C*ame from a poor family*
O*ur hero died of a gun shot wound*
L*og cabin*
N*ever wanted our country to be divided*

Help page for Write On #3

Always A blank person Author of Attempted to Born in Bought Best known for Cared for Came from Could Couldn't Created Died in Did not like Daughter of Even Especially Enemy of Entered Early in life she Famous for First to Father was Formed Friend of Fought for Good at Gave Genuinely tried to Helped Had He Honored for Hurt by	In year he was born Is remembered for Insulted for Insisted on Joined Just because Jealous of Jailed for Joked about Known for King of Kind to Killed by Knew Liked Lived during Learned Loved More Made Married to Mother was Mad about Never noticed Overcame Only Obeyed Ordered Our first Performed Put Probably Quit Quest for Queen of Quite	Respected for Raised in Remembered for Ruled Son of Searched for Studied Sent Said Sad about Taught The person who True to Tried to Trained to Tested Understood Unafraid Unwilling to Voted for Very Went Wanted Was Will be known for Xtra special because Yesterday Years ago she Yes, Younger than Zest for Zealous of

Write On #4
THE FIVE W'S

Objectives
Write descriptive sentences

DIRECTIONS

1. Scribble on your paper without looking at it for four seconds.

2. Look at your design. Can you imagine a picture from the design.

3. Use your pencil to turn your design into that picture.

4. Write a description in three to five sentences. Explain: who, what, where, when, and why.

Make a story out of scribble art.

WHO WHAT WHERE WHEN WHY

This is Mr. Bee. Yesterday he flew to a hive in Georgia to get honey. He gave the honey to his family.

Here is a little silly pink heart. He wants to be a clown at a restaurant when he turns red. He wants to make children laugh.

Work with a partner. After you scribble on the paper, trade papers with your partner.

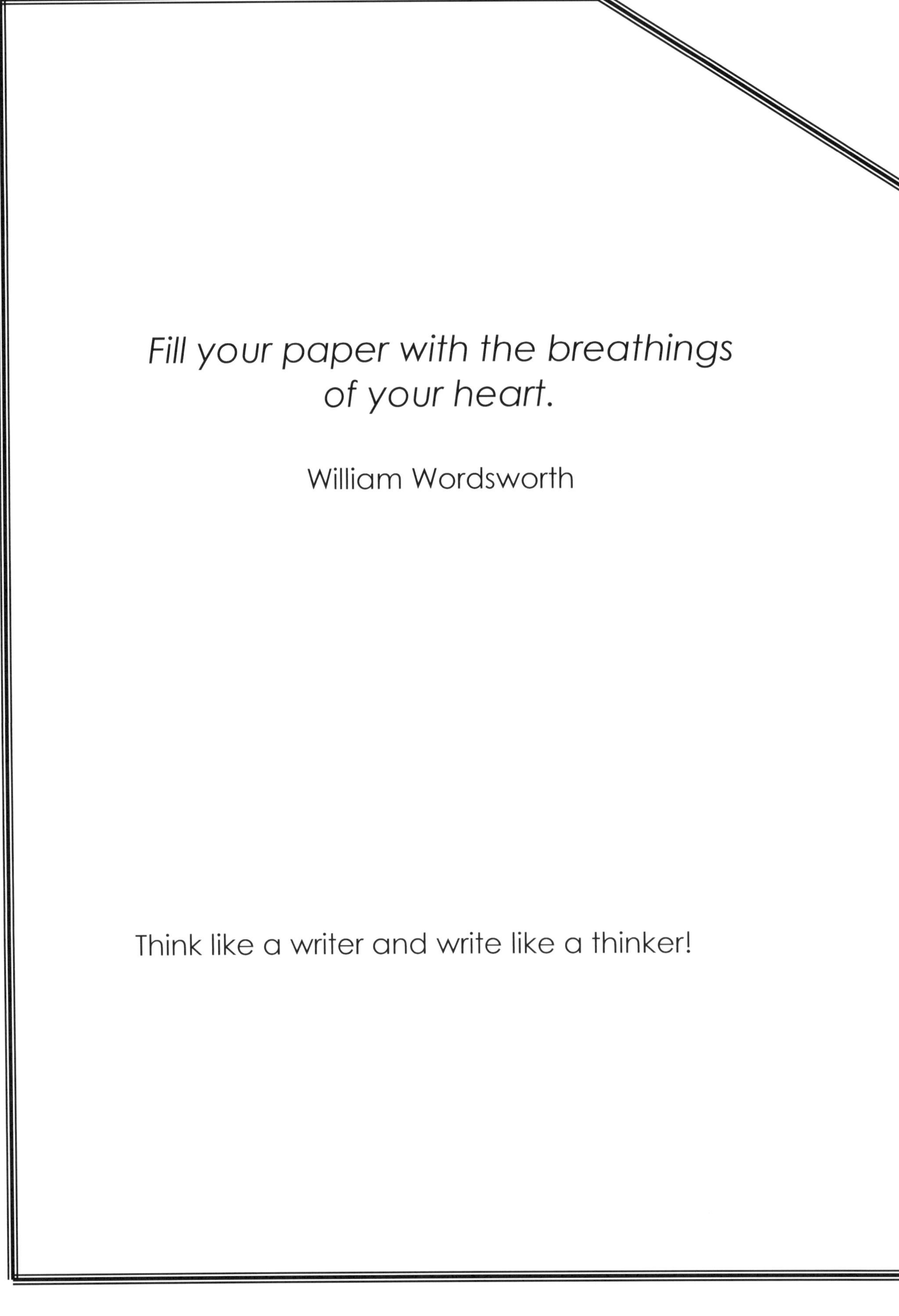

Fill your paper with the breathings of your heart.

William Wordsworth

Think like a writer and write like a thinker!

Objectives

1. *Sentence development*
2. *Compare statements and questions*
3. *Report information*

DIRECTIONS

1. Develop a list of objects, persons, or places from one of your unit studies.

2. For each topic on your list, write three sentences describing it.

3. Write "What am I?" or "Who am I?" after each.

Simple sentences can make a riddle.

1. We have feathers.
   We have a beak.
   Some of us can fly, some can't.
   What are we?

2. We live and breathe under water.
   We are covered with scales.
   We have poor hearing.
   What are we?

3. We hatch from eggs.
   We are scaly, cold-blooded animals.
   We live on land.
   What are we?

4. We live on land and water.
   We are cold-blooded.
   We do not have scales.
   What are we?

5. Most of us are born alive.
   We have hair or fur.
   We stay with our mothers until we are grown.
   What are we?

Answers: 1) birds; 2) fish; 3) reptiles; 4) amphibians; 5) mammals

Write On #6
RHYMING RULES

Objectives

1. Practice rhyming
2. Review contractions
3. Use nouns and verbs

DIRECTIONS

Find verbs and nouns that rhyme. Put them in a sentence with a contraction.

Rhyme Time

Don't tickle the pickle.

Don't pat the cat.

You can't leave your sleeve.

You can't buy money with honey.

I wouldn't thank the bank.

I wouldn't rake a snake.

You couldn't flip a ship.

You couldn't drink a sink.

It's not good to eat wood.

It's not time to rhyme.

Try these starters:
I've never
He's not to
She wouldn't
They'll never
You won't want to

Make an illustrated book

Write On #7
OBVIOUS RULES

Objectives
Creative thinking

DIRECTIONS

1. Imperative sentences are commands.
2. Think of commands that can't be broken.
3. Make them into imperative sentences.

No Signs Allowed!

Do not eat the doorknobs!

No washing hair in the washing machine.

Refrigerator should not be opened before 4 A.M.

Do not bake peanut butter sandwiches in the toaster.

Put your rules on index cards and put them around the house at appropriate locations.

DIRECTIONS

Use information from a history lesson to write a law in your own words.

You are hereby required to write a law.

Act 249 of the British Colonies
The Quartering Act

The American colonists must allow soldiers to enter their homes and reside there. If they resist, their homes shall be confiscated.

Emancipation Proclamation
By Presidential Act 752 of 1863

Slavery is hereby abolished. All slaves are to be set free. Henceforth, America is a free country for all races.

Child Labor Law
Congressional Act 8227

Be it set forth and understood that children under 16 are not to work to support their families. Child labor in all factories is abolished.

Write On #9
THE SHORTEST SENTENCES

Objectives
1 Write simple subject-verb sentences
2 Make longer sentences

DIRECTIONS

1.. List 5 nouns you can see right now. List 5 other nouns that can move. Make your nouns plural.

2. List 5 verbs a puppy can do. List 5 other verbs your father did today.

3. Make 10 noun verb sentences with your lists. Don't forget capitals and periods!

4. You can add more information to make your sentence grow.

The shortest sentences have two words: a subject and a verb.

A noun is a person, place, thing, or idea. If you can touch it, it is a noun.

A verb is an action word. If you can do it, it's a verb.

wall	*walls*	*wiggle*
shoe	*shoes*	*whine*
pencil	*pencils*	*run*
toy	*toys*	*watch*
tree	*trees*	*eat*
car	*cars*	*sleep*
hand	*hands*	*drive*
squirrel	*squirrels*	*talk*
fan	*fans*	*burp*
river	*rivers*	*wash*

Subject-Verb Sentences

Walls wiggle.
Pencils whine.
Shoes run.
Toys watch.
Trees eat.
Cars sleep.
Hands drive.
Squirrels talk.
Fans burp.
Rivers wash.

Growing Sentences

Frisky squirrels talk as they jump from branch to branch.

Some of your sentences may not really make sense. Put a smiley face by those sentences.

Your two word sentence will grow as you add more information. Which sentence is more interesting to read?

Objective

1. Use sentences to describe an object
2. Begin paragraphs

DIRECTIONS

1. Describe an object using complete sentences.

2. Give enough details that someone else will be able to identify the object you described.

Write a description of an object with complete sentences. Can others find the object?

I spy a present under the Christmas tree. It is wrapped in red and white paper. A large bow is on top. Do you think it might be a skateboard?

A bowl of fruit is on the table. There are red and green apples. The bananas are turning brown. Grapes are big and juicy.

This is the tallest tree in the neighborhood. It has green needles and pine cones. Dead brown needles are beneath it. Birds are singing in the branches.

Have someone blindfold you and turn you around several times. When you open your eyes, the first thing you see is what you can describe.

Write On #11
DESCRIBE A SETTING

Objectives
1. Evaluating literature
2. Introduce Write On #14

DIRECTIONS

1. Choose a book you have read.
2. Describe the characters, place and time.
3. Describe the situation the characters face. Complete sentences are not required.

Do you have a favorite book?

Title:	Charlotte's Web
Author:	E.B. Stuart
Main Characters:	Wilbur – a small pig in a farmyard
	Charlotte – an amazing spider who can write words into her web
Place:	the pig pen of an American family farm
Time:	around the 1950's
Situation:	Wilbur will be sold to be butchered soon, but he doesn't want to die. Charlotte uses her incredible writing ability to devise a plan to save Wilbur's life.

Titles of books are underlined. Titles of articles and short stories are in quotation marks. It is easy to remember the difference with this clue: it takes more ink to write a book and to draw a line.

Information can be listed without using complete sentences. Capitals and periods are not required.

Art work can also be used to describe the story.

Objectives
1. Evaluate types of plots
2. Introduce Write On #14

DIRECTIONS

1. Think of several books you have read or movies you have seen. Can you identify the plot?

2. Describe two of each type of plot below that you have read or seen.

3. List two more of each type that you think of yourself.

Stories all have conflicts. The conflict is the problem the main character faces and forms the plot of the story. There are a few common types of plots.

Person vs. Person

A little boy hides from his big sister.
Police try to solve a mystery.
A boat race is held between two friends.
A good guy gets away from a bad guy.

Person vs. Nature

A child tries to walk through a blizzard.
A sick person wants to get well.
A hunter is on a safari with wild animals after him.
A farmer needs rain for his crops to grow.

Person vs. Self

A child must decide if he will be loyal to his friends.
A girl has to make an important decision.
A person has to choose what they will believe.

Objective

1. Develop a plot
2. Introduce Write On #14

DIRECTIONS

1. Decide if the type of story will be realistic fiction or make-believe fiction.

2. List the main characters.

3. Decide what kind of conflict the main character(s) faces.

4 Describe the place and time.

Plot a plot!

Type of Story:	Make-Believe
Main Characters:	a family of talking giraffes
Rolo	the father, who is a bricklayer
Shara	the mother, who works at a candy store
Tara	the sister, who likes to go to the beach
Polo	the main character, who has a sore throat
Conflict:	Person vs. Nature how to get rid of a sore throat
Place:	a make-believe kingdom of talking animals
Time:	modern times - telephones and cars

Write On #14
THREE TRIES STORY

Objectives
Write your fiction story!

DIRECTIONS

1. Many children's stories have three attempts to solve the conflict. Can you think of any stories with three tries?

2. Use the plot you developed in Write On #13. Think of two ways the character(s) may try to solve the conflict without success. Have them succeed on the third attempt.

3. Now, write your story.

Use repetition

1st try – Rolo suggests using mud. It is messy

2nd try – Shara gives him candy. The lollipop stick gets stuck in his throat.

3rd try – Tora takes him to the beach. The salt water helps.

A Long Sore Throat

Polo is a young giraffe. He lives with his mother, father, and sister. Poor Polo has a sore throat. With his long, long neck, a sore throat really hurts.

Polo goes to his father's work. His dad is a brick layer. "My throat hurts. Can you help me?" he asks his father.

His father stops mixing the mud he uses for his bricks. "Mud is soothing. Let's put some on your neck." They put lots of sticky mud on his long neck.

Polo waits for his throat to get better. But the mud dries. It doesn't feel better. "Now I'm a mess, and my throat still hurts," Polo says.

Polo walks to the candy store where his mother works. "My throat hurts. Can you help me?" he asks his mother.

His mother thinks sucking on candy will help his throat. She gives him a lollipop. "Thanks for the lollipop," Polo says.

Polo is walking down the street sucking on his candy. He sucks, then chokes and gasps. "Help me, the lollipop stick is stuck in my throat," he cries. Someone hits him on the back and the stick comes out. "That didn't help," says Polo.

Polo goes to his sister Tara who is going to the beach with her friends. "My throat hurts. Can you help me?" he asks his sister.

"I can't help you, but you can come to the beach with us." Polo goes to the beach. He splashes in the water. He gets his whole neck in the ocean.

Polo gets the water in his mouth. "Help, help, there is salt water in my mouth," he sputters. Polo gargles the salt water. His throat gets better.

"Now my throat is better," says Polo. "Next time I have a sore throat I will gargle with salt water."

Write On #15
THREE SENTENCE REPORT

Objectives
1 Develop an outline
2 Introduce Write On #16

DIRECTIONS

1. Choose an animal.

2. Write three sentences about that animal.

3. The sentences should be independent of each other. (One would not write, "Bees are insects" and "Bees have six legs" because all insects have six legs. Those two sentences are not independent of each other.)

Write 3 different facts.

BEES
1. Bees are insects.
2. They live in hives.
3. Bees make honey.

Tyrannosaurus Rex
1. Tyrannosauraus Rex was large.
2. He was a meat eater.
3. T. Rex had weak front legs.

Penguins
1. Penguins are found in Antarctica.
2. Penguins live in groups.
3. Both parents take care of the young.

Use 3 index cards and cut out the shape of your animal. Write one sentence on each index card.

Make a mobile.

Objectives

1. *Use topic sentences*
2. *Develop paragraphs*
3. *Indent paragraphs*

DIRECTIONS

The sentences from the "Three Sentence Report" will be used.

1. Indent five spaces on your paper. Then write the first sentence from your three sentence report. This is called a topic sentence.

2. Write two to five more sentences telling more about the topic sentence.

3. Indent the next paragraph and write the second sentence from your "Three Sentence Report."

4. Continue the process with the second and third paragraphs.

Each fact becomes a topic sentence.

Tyrannosaurus Rex was a large dinosaur. He was about twenty feet high and his claws were eight inches long. He might have opened his mouth four feet. Tyrannosaurus' head was at least as long as a man.

Tyrannosaurus was a meat eater. His teeth were like daggers. Tyrannosaurus fossils have been found near duck-billed dinosaur fossils. He may have snacked on the duck-bills. He could have eaten other large dinosaurs such as the Apatosaurus.

Tyrannosaurus had weak front legs. They were so short he was not even able to touch his chin. He might have used his front legs as arms to push himself up after a nap. Perhaps Tyrannosaurus used his legs to kill his prey.

Write On #17
POINTS OF VIEW

Objectives
1. *Contrast points of view*
2. *Report information*

DIRECTIONS

1 Choose a subject and list the main objects or people involved.

2. Write a sentence which would identify each.

3. Mix up the order of your lists

Who said it?

1. Slave Owner	A. Slavery is a great evil. It is wicked and cruel.
2. Slave	B. Without slaves our farms and plantations will fail. Who will do the work?
3. Abolitionist	C. I wish I could be free and go to school like the master's children.

1. Flower	**A. How can I be taken out of this flower and turned into honey.**
2. Someone stung by a bee	**B. How much honey have you made today?**
3. Nectar	**C. How am I going to get pollen from another flower to make my seeds?**
4. Bee owner	**D. Ouch! I don't like bees!**

Now, make a quiz for someone else.

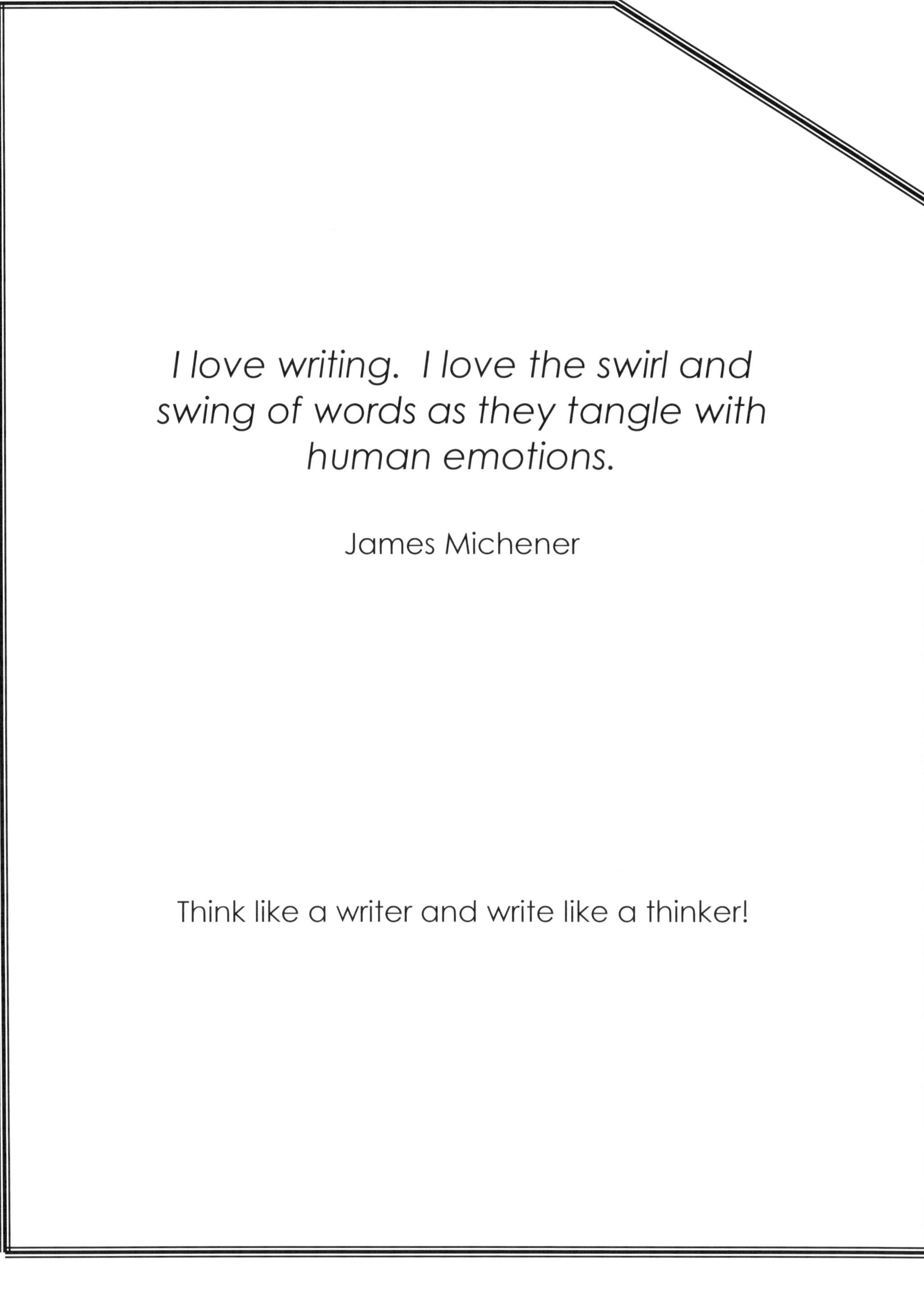

I love writing. I love the swirl and swing of words as they tangle with human emotions.

James Michener

Think like a writer and write like a thinker!

Write On #18
CROSSWORD PUZZLES

Objective
Write vocabulary descriptions

DIRECTIONS

1. Make a list of words from a unit study.

2. Define the words.

3. Place your words on a crossword box so each word intersects with the letters of another word.

4. Number your words and place their definition clues in the DOWN or ACROSS list.

5. Color in the unused boxes.

6. Color in the unused boxes of another blank crossword box to match the one with the letters in it. Give it to someone else to fill in. (Careful, it is easy to make mistakes in coloring in the boxes.)

Do you enjoy crosswords?

Across
1. Drills holes in wood
4. Famous red breast and blue eggs
5. Graceful water bird with long neck
8. United States national bird
9. "Polly wanna cracker!"

Down
2. "Whoo, whoo" (plural)
3. This bright red water bird is the state bird for several states
7. "Quack, quack" (plural

(Answer key on back of this page)

1	2					3					
						4					
	5										
	6										7
			8								
					9						

Use a table in a word processing program to create your crossword box.

Answer Key for Write On #18

1 w	2 o	o	d	p	e	3 c	k	e	r		
	w					a					
	L					4 r	o	b	i	n	
	5 s	w	a	n		d					
						i					
	6 h	u	m	m	i	n	g	b	i	r	7 d
						a					u
			8 e	a	g	l	e				c
											k
					9 p	a	r	r	o	t	s

Write On #19 SPOONERISMS

Objectives
Write spoonerisms

DIRECTIONS

1. Think of some two word expressions. Exchange the first letters. If there is a consonant blend (such as bl or gr) take both letters to the new word.

2. You have a Super Spoonerism if your new words are true words.

3. Write some sentences that have two or more sets of spoonerisms.

Write Spome Soonerisms

Spoonerisms

salt and pepper	palt and sepper
teddy bear	beddy tear
Saturday night	naturday sight
chocolate cake	cocolate chake

Super Spoonerisms

Take a shower	shake a tower
Tea bag	Bea tag
Four cents	Sore fence
Bake a cake	Cake a bake

Spooneriam Sentences
(Or is it Soonerism Spentences?)

How do you nay your same?

I sike to leap with my beddy tear every Naturday sight?

What nind of a kut would write sierd wentences like these?

Write a Tairy Fale

Can you give a spolitical peech?

Think of a description of a gootball fame.

Send a fretter to a lend.

The difference between the almost right word and the right word is really a large matter – it's the difference between the lightning bug and the lightning.

Mark Twain

Think like a writer and write like a thinker!

Write On #20 GATHERING FACTS

DIRECTIONS

1. Make a chart listing "who, what, when, where, why, and how" down the page.

2. Think of different events. Answer the 5 w's for each. Some events may not have one or more parts.

3. Then write sentences with the information.

Objectives

1. ***Write an outline***
2. ***Introduce Write On #21***

Tell the 5 w's.

WHO	Judy, a gorilla	25 year old male	Smith's house	Volcano
WHAT	coming to zoo	robbed a bank	destroyed	erupted
WHEN	tomorrow	last night	Saturday	3 days ago
WHERE	from California	1st National Bank	5th Street	Philippines
WHY	new zoo exhibit	--	--	pressure for six months
HOW	by plane	money from cashier	2 story fire	lava 500 feet high

Judy is a gorilla who is coming all the way from California by plane. She will arrive here tomorrow to join the new exhibit at the Sun Valley Zoo.

A 25 year old man was arrested last night for stealing money from the cash register of the First National Bank.

The Smith's residence was destroyed by fire Saturday night. The two story fire gutted the house on 5th Street. The fire marshal is investigating to determine how the fire started.

Three days ago a volcano erupted in the Philippines for three hours. Pressure had been building for six months which caused the eruption with its 500 foot shower of lava.

Write about:

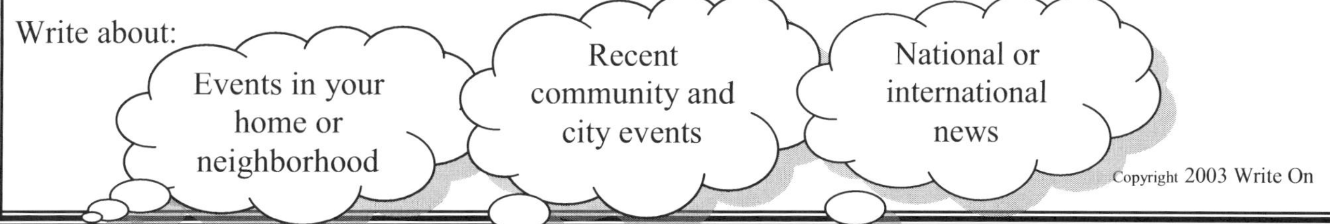

Write On #21
NEWS REPORT

Objectives
1. *Write a news story*
2. *Develop paragraphs*

DIRECTIONS

1. Choose one of the sentences written for Write On #20.

2. Use that sentence as an introductory paragraph.

3. Write a full paragraph giving more information about who, what, where, why, when, or how.

4. Write two or three more paragraphs in the same way.

News reporters tell the 5 W's

WHAT

Judy is a gorilla who is coming all the way from California by plane. She will arrive here tomorrow to join the new exhibit at the Sun Valley Zoo.

WHO

Judy is a 3 year old female gorilla who was born at the zoo in California. She is five feet two inches and weighs 369 pounds. "In spite of her ferocious roar," says zookeeper James Taylor, "Judy is really a very gentle ape."

WHY

The Sun Valley Zoo has been developing a new exhibit for apes. New areas have been made for the chimpanzees and orangutans as well as for Judy. The exhibit is made to look as much as possible like the animals' natural habitat.

WHEN

The new exhibit will be open to the public next Monday. The zoo has spent over a year constructing this site. The animals will be moved into their new area today and tomorrow and given a week to adjust to their new home.

Sometimes "how" is included with the 5 W's.

Objective
Write a poem

DIRECTIONS

1. Choose an adjective.
2. List as many words or phrases as you can to describe it.
3. Arrange your words into a poem.

Some poems describe.

What's Small

Little babies, books, mice,
ears, bees, pebbles,
crumbs, eyelashes,
grains of salt,
dust.

This was written with the largest objects on top.

Color Me Blue

Sky and space
jeans and jay birds
berries and whales
and a sad day

Guess what color this was written in.

It's Dumb!

Wasting money, getting into mischief,
Acting like a fool;
Watching too much TV, being mean,
Trying to be cool.

These were arranged so that the two words that rhymed came at the end of the lines.

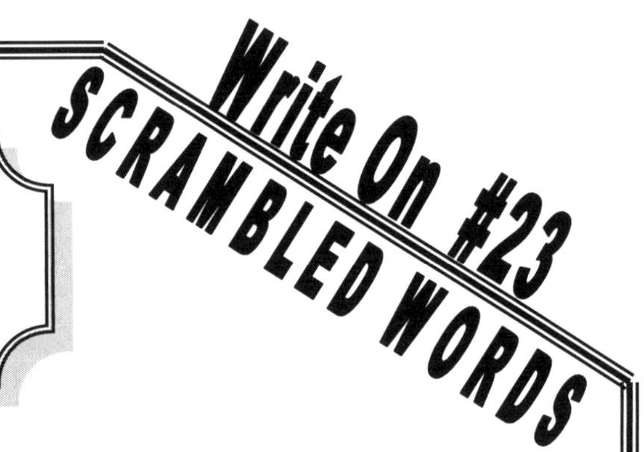

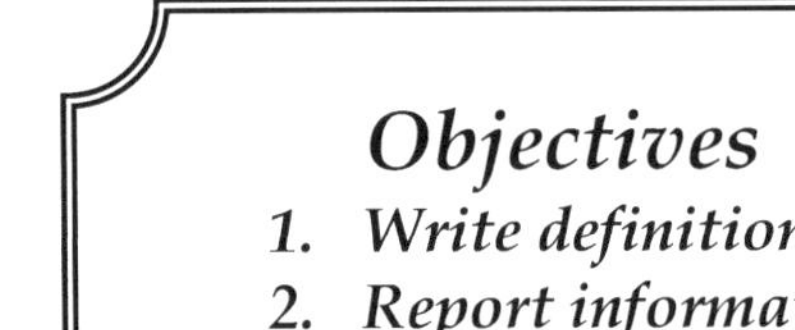

DIRECTIONS

1. Choose vocabulary words from your unit of study.

2. Scramble all the letters in each word.

3. Write a definition for each scrambled word.

ixM up

Unscramble these weather words

1. ITHIDUYM	**large amount of water vapor in the air**
2. EAOPMEHIST	**air that surrounds the Earth**
3. APOVTREAV	**happens when water turns into a cloud**
4. TSLEE	**frozen rain**
5. NWDI	**moving air**
6. TTPPREICINOAI	**falling water**
7. AHLI	**sleet that falls in Spring**
8. GGTLIHENNI	**caused by an electrical current**
9. RRHUICAEEN	**storm over water**

Answers: 1. humidity; 2. atmosphere; 3. evaporate; 4. sleet; 5. wind; 6. precipitation; 7. hail; 8. lightning; 9. hurricane

Write On #24
PRODUCT DESIGN

Objective
Writing slogans

DIRECTIONS

1. Notice the different types of writing script on the commercial packages of products in your kitchen. See if you can imitate the writing of ten different products.

2. Notice if any of the products have slogans.

3. Develop your own product. Include a slogan and script.

4. Can you write an ad for your product?

Become a product engineer.

Made with Pride

We Fry 'Em
You Try 'Em

CRACKLES
CRACKERS

FOR A CRUNCHY GOOD TASTE

What are the serving men?

I keep six honest serving men
They taught me all I knew
Their names are What and Why and When
And How and Where and Who.

Rudyard Kipling

Think like a writer and write like a thinker!

Write On #25
LETTERS

Objectives

1. Letter writing
2. Paragraph development

DIRECTIONS

1. Decide who the letter will be written to.

2. Make a list of the kinds of information you may include in your letter. Look at the topics listed on the side of the sample below.

3. Write one paragraph for each topic. Remember to indent each paragraph.

Do you ever have trouble knowing what to say in a letter?

	Dear Chris,
Respond to one of their letters	*Thanks for your letter. It's hard to believe you have so much snow when we have warm weather here.*
Something you have done or are planning	*Last week we went hiking. It took us half the day. I'm looking forward to summer when our family goes camping. Do you like to camp?*
News about a friend or relative	*I have a friend, Andy, who was hurt playing football. His leg will be in a cast for four weeks or more. We prayed for him in Sunday School.*
What you are doing in school	*In school I am studying space. I did a report on the eclipse. We are planning on making a model of the solar system. When we are done it will be spread across my whole room. Earth will be a ping pong ball. I think space is amazing to study.*
Something happening right now (even if it is trivial)	*My mom has brownies cooking. Yum! I hope we have vanilla ice cream to put on top.*
Something you have done or an interest you share	*The model plane we worked on together is still on the shelf in my room. Have you made any more models lately? I'm saving my money for this cool ship I saw at the store. Maybe if you visit again this summer, we can work on it together.*
	Your friend,,
	Steven

Write On #26
HISTORICAL LETTERS

Objectives

1. *Gather facts*
2. *Report information*

DIRECTIONS

1. Gather facts from a history lesson.

2. Pretend you are living in that time. Write a letter from one person to another using the facts you gathered.

3. The characters may be true or fictitious.

You can write fictitious letters to tell what happened in history.

Dear Ben,

I'm at Valley Forge because it is snowing and our army can't travel well in the snow. The other reason we are camped out here is that it's a safe spot to defend against an attack by the British. There are natural hills and mountains and a river to help us in case of an attack. We are just a few miles outside of Philadelphia where the British soldiers are staying in the homes of the people.

We have built log cabins to stay in. Twelve men stay in one small cabin. We sleep on wooden boards covered with hay. There is very little food to go around. Many of our soldiers are dying from sickness. Please tell the people in our village how much we need them to send us food and supplies.

Your brother,

Dear Queen Isabelle,

I wanted to write and again ask for your help to find a new way to the Orient. As I told you in person, I am sure the world is round and shaped like a ball. We can sail across the ball without falling off. I have studied all the maps and navigated many ships. It will be much quicker to sail straight across the ocean than to sail south of Africa and around. I will need several ships to make the journey. Although the King of Portugal would not help, I am sure you realize how much this would mean to Spain to have a faster route to the East.

Your humble servant,

Christopher Columbus

Your library may have some interesting history books that are written as letters or fiction.

Objectives
Write dialogues
Introduce Write On #28

DIRECTIONS

1. Think of an answer to the question, "What do you have there?"

2. Write your answer in different dialects.

People of different dialects will say things differently.

"What do you have there?"

Formal:	"What, may I be so bold to ask, is it that you have there?"
Baby:	"Lemme see dat."
Old English	"What, pray tell, havest thou?"
Southern	"What do ya' all have?"
Careless English	"Whatcha got?"
Slang:	"Man alive! What's that?"

Write a conversation between two people with different dialects.

Rewrite a paragraph from a book using the dialect from a favorite character of another book or movie.

Write On #28
DIALOGUES FROM DAYS GONE BY

Objectives
1. Write dialogues
2. Report information

DIRECTIONS

1. Make notes from your history lesson of facts about that period.

2. Develop a dialogue. The characters can be real or made up. Have them discuss the facts you listed.

3. Include the accents of the character's dialogue.

Tell about something that happened in history, using the accents from that era.

NOTES

Pioneers – first to go to a new place
- Some wanted a new life.
- Get away from crowds
- Others stayed home – afraid of Indians

Daniel Boone led 30 men with axes.
- Made path through wooded mountains
- Path was called "Wilderness Trail"

Smitty: "What's this I hear tell 'bout you taking a posse of men and headin' fer the West?"

Daniel: "You've heard right. I'm going to cross the mountains to find a way for people to move to Kentucy."

Smitty: "Why yore plum crazy? No one kin git 'cross them mountains. Why the trees is thicker th'n molasses and thar tain't no path either. Even if thar was, its straight ways up the side of one mountain and straight ways down the other side. It's nothin' but a waste of time to try and cross 'em."

Daniel: "I'm leading a group of men and we are going to clear a path through those trees with our axes. We'll find the easiest mountains and valleys to cross. And we are going to cross them!"

Smitty: "Why for? There ain't no stores, no farms, no doctors, not a bit of civilization. All you's gonna find is hardships and Indians and all kinds of trouble. Even if you do make a trail and build yerself a cabin out in that wilderness, not a single living woman's gonna go out thar."

Daniel: "Smitty, once we get a trail cleared men will settle the West. Then families can come out in wagons on the trails we have made."

Smitty: "All a bunch of hogwash! No one wants that wilderness. You jist listen to me and stay put. Otherwise yore gonna be the laughin' stock fer years to come."

Write On #29
TRUE CLUES

Objectives
1. Write creative definitions
2. Practice rhyming

DIRECTIONS

1. Think of two words that rhyme.

2. Write a description of the rhyming phrase. Neither of the two words can be in the description.

3. Make a list.

4. Give your definitions to someone without the rhyming words. Can they guess what the words are?

Beware: If you do this all day you might become a word nerd.

Sweet beet	*a red vegetable cooked in sugar*
Phony pony	*a fake horse*
Sea tea	*drink made from ocean water*
Red bed	*scarlet colored furniture to sleep on*
Shoe glue	*sticky stuff that holds boots together*
Eagle beagle	*cross between the American bird and a dog*
Farm alarm	*a rooster that crows when there is trouble*
Fake snake	*a rubber serpent*

Have you heard a picture is worth a thousand words? What do you think of this statement?

In a thousand words I can have the Lord's Prayer, the 23rd Psalm, the Hippocratic Oath, a sonnet by Shakespeare, the Preamble to the Constitution, Lincoln's Gettysburg Address and almost all of the Boy Scout Oath. Now exactly what picture were you planning to trade for all that?

Roy H. Williams

Think like a writer and write like a thinker!

Write On #30
Pros and Cons

Objective
Organize ideas

DIRECTIONS

Choose an unusual activity. Develop a list of ten pros and ten cons.

Cons – Reasons against

Buying a pet elephant

Pros	Cons
You will never need a tow truck.	**He will be expensive to feed.**
He will scare burglars away.	**He might step on Mom's flowers.**
He can squirt you in hot weather.	**He can't curl up at the foot of your bed.**
None of your friends will have one.	**He might scare the other animals in the vet's office.**
You can have your own neighborhood circus.	**They stink.**
He can help you put up your tent when you are camping.	**It will be hard to cut his toe nails with regular clippers.**
You can sell elephant rides to raise money for charity.	**He might knock down your tent when you are camping.**
He'll protect you from bullies.	**He might step on your foot when you take him for a walk.**
He can vacuum your carpet.	**He won't fit in your wading pool.**
He can eat all the leftovers.	**You might get a backache trying to lift him.**

Do the advantages OUTWEIGH the disadvantages?

Try these ideas:
Owning a lion
Taking a vacation in a balloon
A gold mine in your back yard
Your Mom is president.

Write sentences about:

Your home

What you did today

Your history lesson

A friend

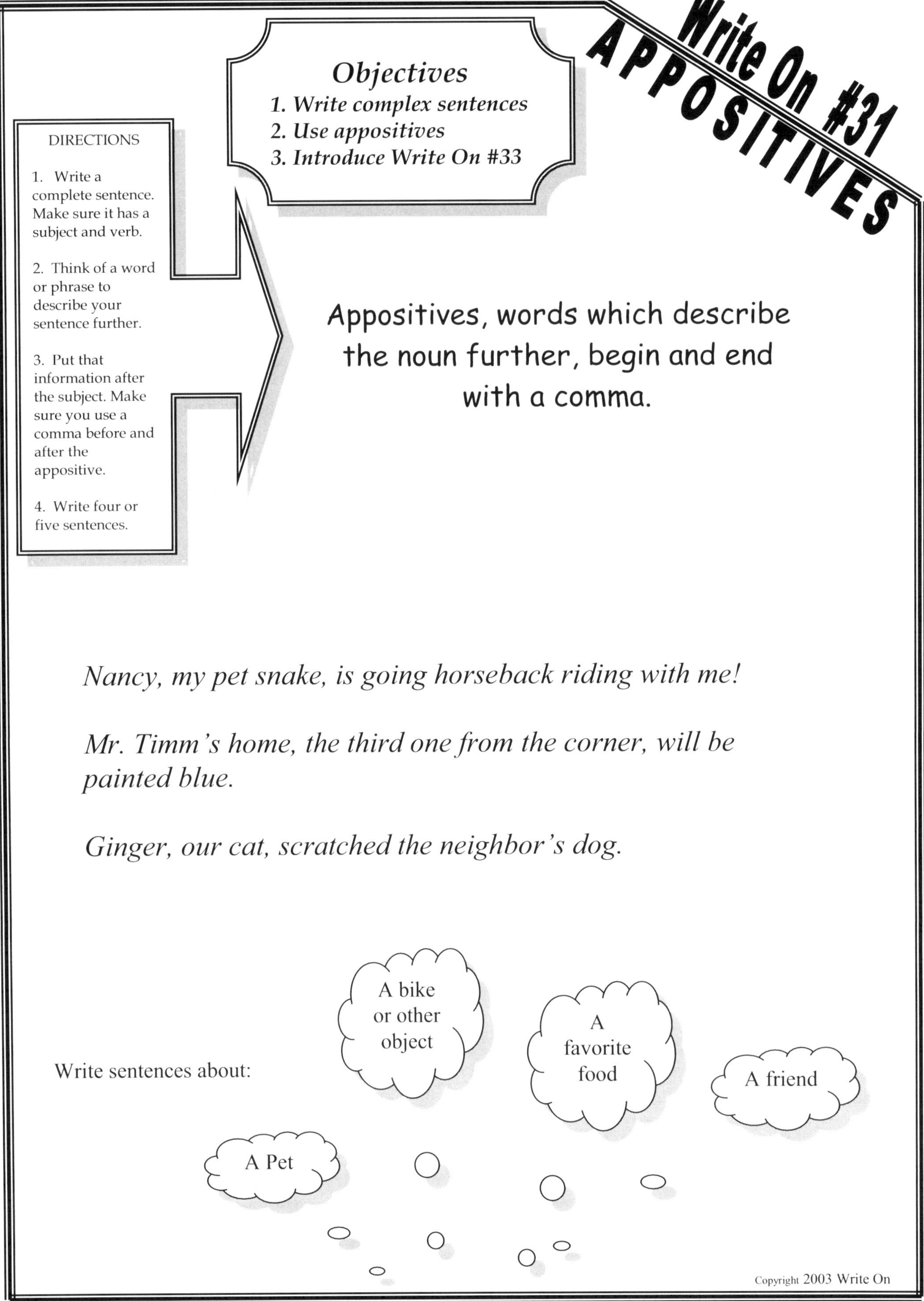
Write On #31
APPOSITIVES
Objectives
1. Write complex sentences
2. Use appositives
3. Introduce Write On #33
DIRECTIONS
1. Write a complete sentence. Make sure it has a subject and verb.
2. Think of a word or phrase to describe your sentence further.
3. Put that information after the subject. Make sure you use a comma before and after the appositive.
4. Write four or five sentences.
Appositives, words which describe the noun further, begin and end with a comma.
Nancy, my pet snake, is going horseback riding with me!
Mr. Timm's home, the third one from the corner, will be painted blue.
Ginger, our cat, scratched the neighbor's dog.
Write sentences about:
A bike or other object
A favorite food
A friend
A Pet
Copyright 2003 Write On

Write On #32
SEMICOLONS
Objectives
1. Write complex sentences
2. Use semicolons in a complex sentence
3. Introduce Write On #33
DIRECTIONS
1. Think of something someone might need to do. Write it as a complete sentence.
2. Give more information about why. Write it as a complete sentence. The two sentences should express one thought or idea.
3. Use a semicolon between the two sentences.
4. Write four of these sentences.
These are two complete sentences; a semicolon is used.
My plane is leaving; I have to run.
Call 911; there's a fire.
Don't eat that; it is poisonous.
Write sentences about:
Something dangerous
A chore or assignment
A future plan
Your father's job

Write On #33
COMPLEX SENTENCES

Objective
Write complex sentences

DIRECTIONS

1. Choose a topic.
2. Write a simple sentence about your topic. This will tell what your paragraph is about.
3. Write a sentence that starts with a dependent clause to give more information about this topic.
4. Write one more sentence. Use an appositive to describe the subject further.

Use different types of sentences in a paragraph.

A sentence is a complete thought. Although a sentence may be complex, it still communicates one central thought. Certain sentences, which have appositives, give additional information in a parenthetical way.

We have a cockatiel. Since cockatiels are social birds, they demand a lot of attention. Our bird, named Sunburst, is just like a member of our family.

Jan is my friend. Because she lives next door, I see her almost every day. We often talk about things, like our dreams, which are important to us.

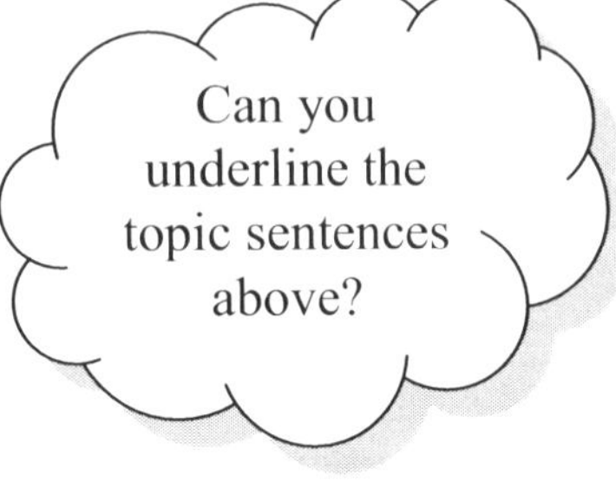

Objectives

1. Practice alliteration
2. Use rhyming

DIRECTIONS

1. Develop phrases that have alliteration.

2. Keep your list. You may use some of the phrases in your writing later on.

Rhyming words end alike. (hat, cat)
Words with alliteration start with the same sound. (King Kong)

Chocolate chip cheese cake

Smirky smiles

Perfectly patterned pretzels

A shabby shoe shiner

waiting...wondering...watching

Aggravating aggravations

Please pass the pumpkin patch.

Use alliterations for:
Poetry
Name of a business
Titles of books or articles
Describe a place or person

We are all apprentices in a craft where no one ever becomes a master.

Ernest Hemingway

Think like a writer and write like a thinker!

Objectives

1. Organize thoughts
2. Introduce Write On #36

DIRECTIONS

1. Think of an activity someone can do.

2. Write step by step directions in the order each step needs to be done.

3. Do this for three other activities.

Do you like to give directions?

How to Make Scrambled Eggs

1. **Gather supplies**
2. **Crack eggs in the bowl**
3. **Mix in the milk**
4. **Fry them in the skillet**

How to Plan a Party

1. **Choose a party theme**
2. **Make a guest list**
3. **Plan the menu**
4. **Plan the activities**
5. **Invite your guests**
6. **Get your house ready**

Objectives

1. Write topic sentences

2. Develop paragraphs into an essay

DIRECTIONS

1 Choose one of the activities from Write On #35. The steps will become your outline.

2. For each step, write a complete sentence. This will be the topic sentence for your paragraph.

3. After each sentence, give a more detailed explanation with two to five additional sentences. This will be your paragraph.

4. Complete this process for each step.

An essay can give directions on how to do something.

Scrambled Eggs

Do you ever wake up in the morning hoping for scrambled eggs? I do. And since I learned how to make them, I can have them whenever I want.

First you have to gather the supplies. A frying pan is needed, and margarine or oil to melt in the bottom of the pan. We need a bowl to crack the eggs in and another to hold them in. Milk is also in scrambled eggs. And don't forget the eggs!

Each egg should be cracked individually in a separate bowl. Sometimes an egg is bad or pieces of the shell fall in. By having a separate bowl, you don't mess up any of the other eggs.

Once the eggs are cracked, milk is mixed in. I use ¼ cup of milk with three eggs. Beat them together until they are well mixed.

Next, pour the mixture into the frying pan and turn the heat to medium. It's important to keep turning and scrambling the egg mixture or it will burn.

Finally, I serve them on a plate. Sometimes I add ketchup. Some people like to use salt and pepper.

Write On #37
INTRODUCE & CONCLUDE

Objective
Write introductions and conclusions

DIRECTIONS

1. Use the steps you wrote for one of the directions in Write On #35. Or you may want to write steps to a new activity instead.

2. Write a one paragraph introduction, telling the reader what the essay is about.

3. Finish your essay with a one paragraph conclusion.

An interesting introduction and conclusion makes your essay more enjoyable to read.

Travel Safely

Honk! Screech! CRASH! Those horrible sounds are heard by somebody every day. There are four things you can do to prevent yourself from being injured in a car accident.

1) Avoid traveling in bad weather
2) Obey traffic rules
3) Watch out for others on the road
4) Always wear your seat belt

No one wants to be injured in a car accident. If you avoid traveling in bad weather, obey traffic rules, watch out for others, and always wear your seat belt; you may prevent an accident that could cost your life. So if you have some place you want to go, do everything you can to make sure you get there.

Write On #38
BOOK REPORTS

Objective
Write a book report

DIRECTIONS

1. Write one or two paragraphs on what the book was about.

2. What was the author's goal? Was it accomplished?

3. Give your evaluation of the book. Tell its strengths and weaknesses.

4. Tell who might like to read this book.

After reading a book, write a report about it. Those who read your report may decide to read the book themselves, or they may decide it is not a book they want to read.

Find the Constellations is a book by H.A. Rey about the constellations. It introduces the reader to the major constellations in the first part of the book. Quizzes are also provided to review each constellation. In the second part, four different sky-views are shown: one for each season. There is also a planet finder and time table.

The purpose of the book is to teach about the night sky. The book describes its purpose on the first page. "At night time, when the stars are out, the sky all of a sudden becomes a huge Picture Book. You can look up and see a lion and a whale, an eagle, a swan, a dog, a hare, and a lot of other pictures; that is of course if you know how to find them. Those pictures are made by the Stars, and finding them is a wonderful game. Let us start the game…."

Cartoons and drawings are used to illustrate the book. They make the book fun and easy to read.

The book not only discusses the stars, but also gives information on the sun and planets. But it does not talk about the moon. It would have been good if that was covered as well.

Find the Constellations is a good book for someone who wants to learn about the sky. It is not like a textbook. Stories about some of the constellations are included, as well as the scientific facts. Learning is easy and fun with this book.

Write On #39
OPPOSITES IN RHYME

Objectives
1. Write poetry
2. Creative thinking

DIRECTIONS

1. Make a list of words or phrases that mean wrong.
Such as:
upside down
mixed up
gone bonkers

2. Find rhymes to go with your phrases:
upside down & turned around
off its track & out of whack
out of sync & missing a link

3 . Make another list of words that rhyme:
old/cold
top/stop

4. Find the opposite of those words to make couplets
hot, cold
young, old
or
go, stop
bottom, top

Mix and match an opposing batch.

If cold was hot and hot was cold,
And old was young and young was old;
And down was up and up was down,
Then I'd think everything was upside down.

If downstairs was put on the upper floor,
And the inside was taken out the door;
And the country was in the middle of the town,
Then I'd think everything was upside down.
And if everything was upside down,
and inside out,
and all mixed up,
and turned around,
Would I know what ought to be?
Or would I think that you were me?

I love being a writer. What I can't stand is the paperwork.

Peter De Vries

Writing is easy. All you do is sit staring at a blank sheet of paper until drops of blood form on your forehead.

Gene Fowler

Think like a writer and write like a thinker!

1. Begin an outline
2. Introduce Write On #41

DIRECTIONS

1. Choose a topic.
2. Brainstorm ten advantages to your topic.

Make a list of advantages as quickly as you can. You can do this with others. This is called brainstorming.

Advantages of Knowing How to Do Math

1. Save money
2. Figure gas mileage
3. Tithe
4. Buy things at the store
5. Carpentry and woodworking
6. Use recipes
7. Sports player's scores
8. Balance checkbook
9. Sewing
10. Games

You might want to list advantages to one of these topics:

Write On #41
ADVANTAGES ESSAY

DIRECTIONS

Use your list of advantages from Write On #40

Step One
Organize your ideas by grouping them around common ideas. Some things may be changed, deleted, or added. This will be your outline for your essay.

Step Two
From each point of your outline, write a complete sentence. This will be your topic sentence.

Step Three
For each topic sentence, develop a paragraph.

Objectives
1. Outlining
2. Paragraph and essay

Your list of advantages will help you write an essay.

Step One

MONEY
Save money
Tithe
Buy things
Balance checkbook

JOBS
Carpenters
Seamstress
Cooks
Truck drivers

FUN
Sports
Games
Arts and crafts

Step Two

1. Math is important to anyone who uses money.

2. Many jobs require math.

3. Math is useful for having fun.

Step Three

Math is important to anyone who uses money. In order to save or count your money you need to know math. If someone does not know how to add or subtract, they cannot buy anything at a store. In order to pay our tithe or balance our checkbook, math is needed.

Many jobs require math. A carpenter has to know how much wood to cut. To sew a dress, a seamstress has to cut out the right amount of material. Cooks use math to figure the right amount of ingredients in their recipes. And a truck driver needs to know how many miles he can go on a tank of gas.

Math is useful for having fun. Sportsmen use math to keep scores. Even playing a board game requires using numbers to keep track of points. Some arts and crafts projects use math. There are so many things we could not do if we didn't know math.

Write On #42
WORD SUBSTITUTES

Objectives

1. Eliminate over-used words.
2. Use a thesaurus
3. Introduce Write On #43

DIRECTIONS

1. Choose a common word. You may want to use one of these:
   - look
   - went
   - big
   - nice
   - want

2. With another person or persons, take ten minutes to list other words or phrases that could be used instead.

3. Use a thesaurus to come up with additional synonyms.

4. Look for other words and phrases in your reading.

Which of these statements sounds more interesting?

He went out quickly.
OR
He scrambled out of there with lightning speed.

SAID	GOT	SMALL
Explained	**Ended up with**	**Miniature**
Hollered	**Inherited**	**Tiny**
Answered	**Bought**	**Itsy bitsy**
Mentioned	**Took out**	**Lesser**
Responded	**Acquired**	**Tad bit**
Whispered	**Purchased**	**Microscopic**
Exclaimed	**Found**	**Measly**
Replied	**Was given**	**Insignificant**
Complained	**Brought home**	**Undersized**
Declared	**Came up with**	**Reduced**

String a line across the room. Use index cards and clothes pins to hang up any word substitutes you think of or find.

Tape three common words to the outside of three different cups. For one week, everyone puts any substitute words into the right cup. See which cup has the most.

Write On #43
SAY IT AGAIN

Objective
Write dialogue

DIRECTIONS

1. Make a Word Substitute list for the word "said."

2. Make another list for the word "yes" or "maybe."

3. Match the words from one list to the words in another. This may be by random selection or by choice.

4. Write dialogue lines. To add variety, place the speech tag in the front of some quotes, at the end or middle of others.

How many ways can you say, "NO"?.

"No," said Linda.

"Not a chance," Linda exclaimed.

Linda hollered, "No way!"

"Not again," complained Linda.

"Never, " Linda whispered in a hoarse voice, "never."

"Not by the hair of my chinny chin chin," responded Linda.

"The answer," declared Linda, "is absolutely no!"

Linda answered in a surprised voice, "You've got to be kidding!."

Read your sentences out loud. Try to change the expression in your voice to match the dialogue.

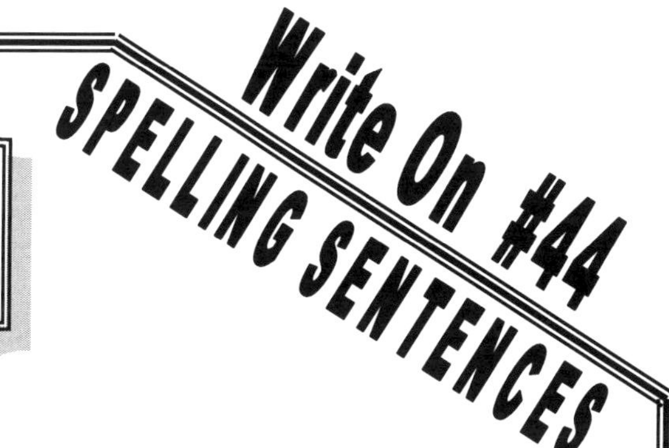

Objective
Have fun using spelling or vocabulary words in sentences

DIRECTIONS

1. Use your spelling or vocabulary list for this Write On.

2. Write sentences with at least three spelling words in each sentence.

3. Write the words in any order.

The spelling words are bolded. Do you think you would have come up with entirely different sentences if this was your spelling list?

The **perfect judge announced** he would not enter the **cathedral** unless a **thorough** search of the **cellar** was made.

The **chief** expressed a **complaint** about the **temperature** of the **palace.**

The captives **entertained** themselves **repairing** a **section** of rope to **enable** them to **escape.**

Our **company,** which had **traveled** the **entire distance,** was **weary.**

You can take for granted that people know more or less what a street, a shop, a beach, a sky an oak tree look like. Tell them what makes this one different.

Neil Gaiman

Think like a writer and write like a thinker!

Write On #45
DESCRIPTIVE OUTLINES

Objectives

1. *Compare concept maps and vertical outlines*
2. *Make an outline and concept map*
3. *Introduce Write On #46*

DIRECTIONS

1. Choose a topic you have been studying.

2. Use a concept map and a vertical outline to list several of the 5 W's (who, what, when, where, why & how).

Some students use a concept map to develop their outlines. Others like to use a vertical outline. Which do you prefer?

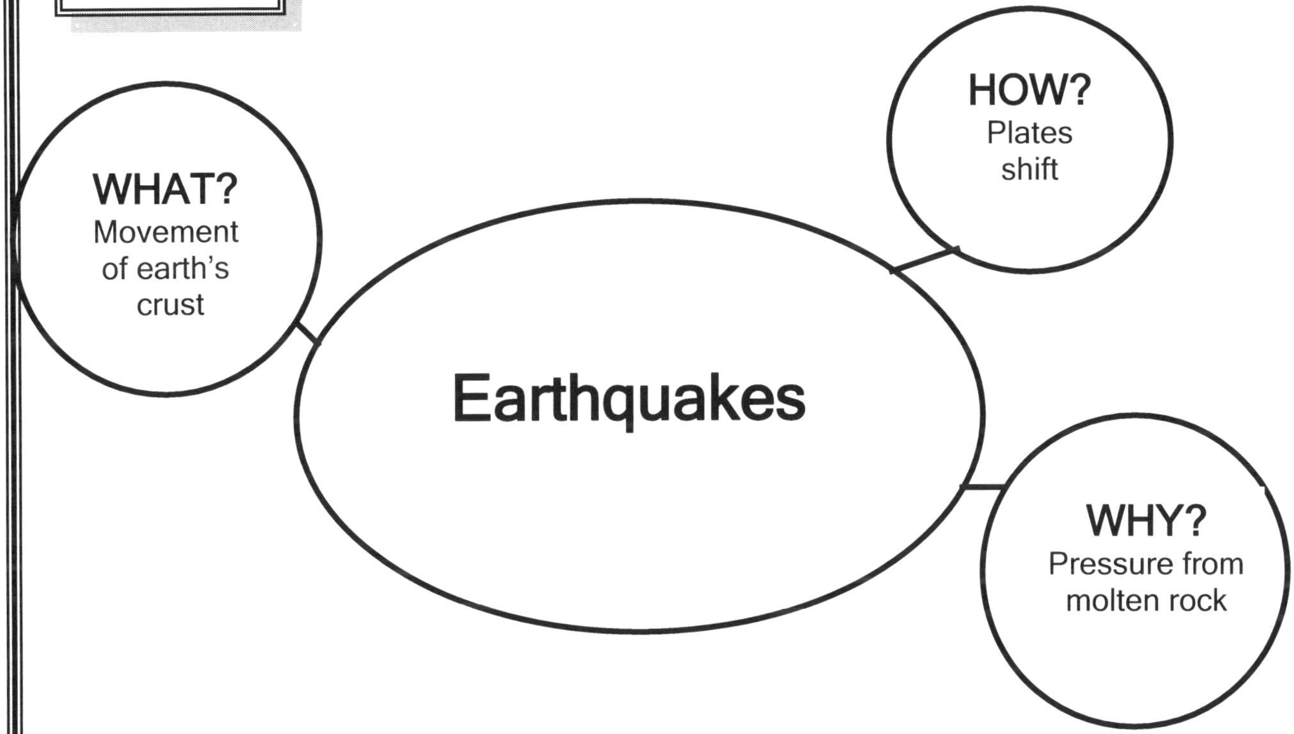

Earthquakes

WHAT?
Movement of earth's crust

HOW?
Plates shift

WHY?
Pressure from molten rock

Earthquakes Outline

What: Movement of earth's crust
How: Plates shift
Why: Pressure from molten rock

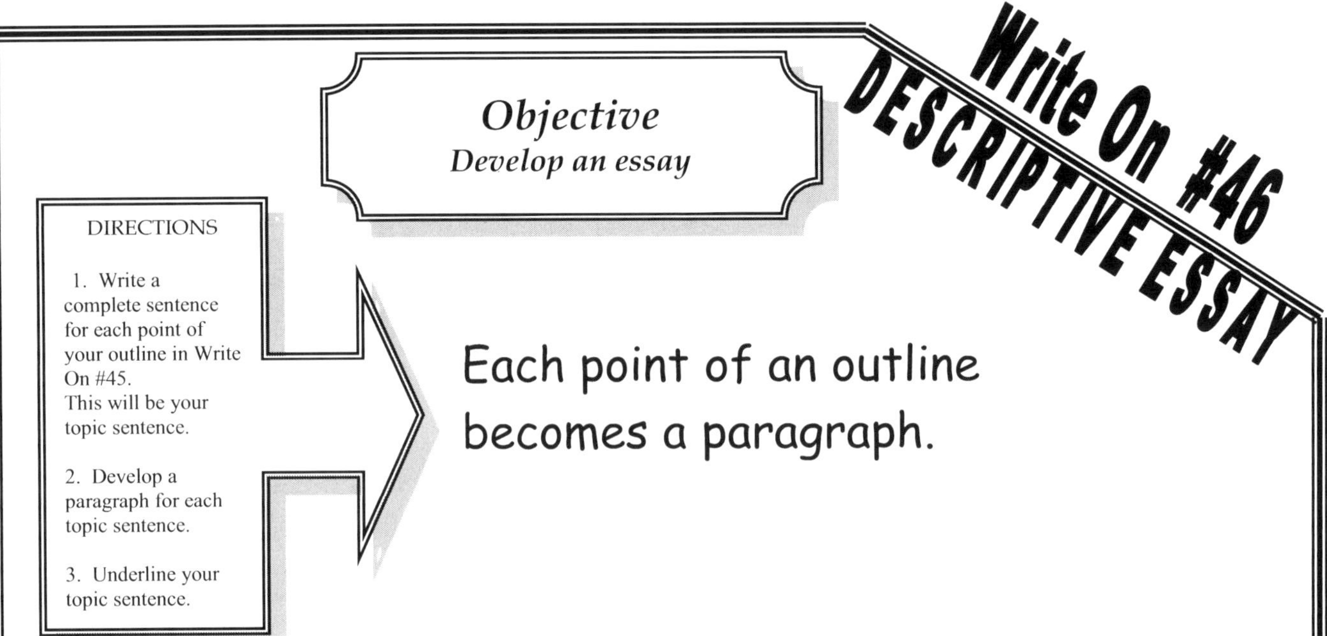

EARTHQUAKES

An earthquake is a movement of the earth's crust. When the crust moves, it causes the ground to shake and tremble. Earthquakes cause buildings and bridges to collapse when the earth moves.

This movement is caused by shifts in the plates of the earth. Imagine you have crackers on a table top, and some of the crackers are touching each other. The edges of some crackers are on top of one another, and a few have spaces in between them. If dirt covered the top of the crackers, the dirt would move if the crackers were moved. Although we cannot see the plates under the ground, the ground still shakes when the plates are moved.

The plates are moved by the pressure of molten rock below the earth's crust. This is the same molten rock that shoots out of volcanoes. Far beneath the surface of the earth there is an ocean of molten rock. There are currents in the molten rock similar to the currents in the seas. These currents put pressure on the earth's plates. And when the plates begin to shift: watch out!

Write On #47
HOUSES FOR SALE

Objective
Descriptive writing

DIRECTIONS

1. Read the real estate section of the classified ads. Notice the variety some realtors use in the opening sentences or closing sentences.

2. Write a short ad for your house.

3. Write a longer ad for your house describing it in more detail.

4. Check the prices for the classified ads. How much would it cost to put the two different ads in?

Write a classified ad for your house.

For Sale

Your family will be thrilled with this two story house with a finished basement. Two small bedrooms and one large master bedroom are perfect for a family. Kids will love the large backyard. Nice one car garage. Call 219-4102. $169,000

For sale:
Three bedroom house with garage and finished basement. 2 stories. Call 830-0030.

Now write an ad for your dream house!

Do not put statements in the negative form.

And don't start sentences with a conjunction.

If you reread your work, you will find on rereading that a great deal of repetition can be avoided by rereading and editing.

Never use a long word when a diminutive one will do.

Unqualified superlatives are the worst of all.

De-accession euphemisms.

If any word is improper at the end of a sentence, a linking verb is.

Avoid trendy locutions that sound flaky.

Last, but not least, avoid cliches like the plague.
~William Safire

Think like a writer and write like a thinker!

Write On #48
Smile, It's a Simile

DIRECTIONS

1. Brainstorm a list of similes that use "as" or "like" to compare two things.

2. Write longer similes that are complete sentences.

3. Look for opportunities in your writing to use similes.

Objective
Create similes.

Similes compare two things.
They have "like" or "as" in them.

yellow as a buttercup

happy as a puppy in a big yard

silly as a monkey

fun as a trip to Disneyland

scary as a dark moonless night

rich as a millionaire

clouds like cotton candy

a row of houses like kids' blocks

her voice sounds like a harp

heart that was hard as a rock

trouble came like waves

perfect like a picture

LONGER SIMILES

Swimming in the river is like
diving into a pool of whipped cream.

A field trip is like
taking a one day vacation.

A card from Grandma is like
a hug in the mail.

Eating hot dogs on the porch is like
having an indoor picnic.

Write On #49
EVER MET A METAPHOR?

DIRECTIONS

1. Metaphors are similar to similes but do not contain the words "as" or "like".

2. Rearrange the words in your similes to make metaphors.

3. Write three sentences with metaphors.

4. For each expression, decide if you feel a simile or metaphor is more effective.

Objective
Write metaphors

A metaphor is a picture and a thought entwined together.

cotton candy clouds

waves of trouble

monkey silly

picture perfect

buttercup yellow

Heart of Rock

Her sky blue eyes smiled at me.

Write On #50
QUOTATION RULES

Objective
Use punctuation with quotation marks correctly

DIRECTIONS

Find a book or magazine with dialogue that you can mark in.

1. Underline everything that is spoken with blue.

2. Put a green checkmark at each paragraph when a new speaker is speaking.

3. Find the punctuation at the beginning and end of each quote. Circle the punctuation with red.

4. Notice how the speaker may be identified before the quote, after it, or in the middle of it. Underline the identification of the speaker in orange. Mark "B" over it if the speaker is identified **before** the quote; "A" if the identification is **after** the quote; and "M" if it is in the **middl**e.

Four Important Rules

1. Everything that is spoken must be in quotation marks.

2. Each new speaker begins a new paragraph. The paragraph must be indented.

3. In addition to the quotation mark, there is punctuation before and after each quote. It may be a capital letter, a comma, period or question mark.

4. To give variety, the speaker may be identified before the quote, after it, or in the middle of it.

Dialogue on Quotations

My teacher told us, "In addition to the quotation marks, every sentence will also begin and end with punctuation."

Tom was confused, "What if the quote is a complete sentence?" he asked.

"That is very easy. There is a capital at the beginning of the sentence, and there is a period or question mark at the end of the sentence," she explained.

"But what do you do," asked Mike, "if the sentence is broken up in the middle to tell who is speaking?"

"That is not a problem," she answered, "because you use commas before and after the interruption."

Bob had more information. "Don't forget that each time a new speaker speaks, the writer needs to change paragraphs. A paragraph can include several sentences. Or it may only have one word."

"Really?"

"Yes, a paragraph needs only one word if that is all the speaker said," our teacher responded. "But you must remember to indent each paragraph, no matter how long or short."

"I guess writing quotations isn't difficult after all," mused Tom. "And the dialogue does make information more interesting to read."

A metaphor is like a simile.

Author Unknown

Metaphors have a way of holding the most truth in the least space.

Orson Scott Card

Think like a writer and write like a thinker!

Write On #51
QUOTES & DIALOGUES

Objective
Write a dialogue

DIRECTIONS

1. Write a dialogue between two or more characters.

2. Make sure you follow the rules for quotations.

3. It takes longer to write passages with dialogue. But don't you agree it is more interesting to read? What would your favorite story be like if the author did not include dialogue?

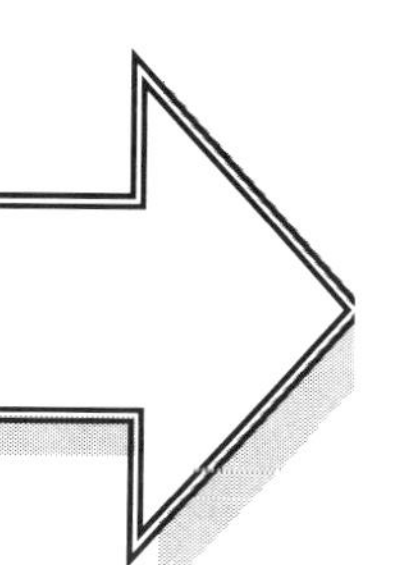

Dialogue makes your stories come alive.

Dinosaur Adventure

John, the cave man, sat on a rock impatiently waiting for his young duck billed dinosaur to get trained. While he was working with Ducky-Ducky, the dinosaur ran out of sight.

"I wonder what got into him," John said as he sat with his training stick in the same position as if he were still training Ducky-Ducky.

"I haven't the slightest idea why he ran away. But I do know that crazy critter of yours, as dumb as he is, would have a half decent reason for taking off like that," Bill said. Bill was John's friend who often teased him about his pet dinosaur.

"Hey! Would you stop teasing me about my pet and help find Ducky?" John asked.

They both ran at least a mile and Bill was already tired.

"Just forget about your beast. I just can't run like this anymore," Bill complained.

"Well, I hope you can walk because we're going to walk through this cave and look for Ducky." They were silent as they crept into the dark cave. Then all of a sudden a horrible noise broke the silence. "RRRRRoarrrrr," came a noise from inside the cave.

"Yikes!" Bill said as he hid behind John. "What was that?"(continued next page)

Ideas for your dialogues:

- Aliens in a grocery store
- Two kids buying a present for Grandma
- A cat telling a puppy about his new home
- A trip in a hot air balloon
- Finding a secret treasure
- The brain talking to the heart while the person sleeps

"I don't know, but I do know it would be smart to get out of here!" John answered. When they both darted from the cave they saw a twenty foot high lizard with a body forty feet long. In its mouth were teeth a foot tall and as sharp as daggers. The beast glared at them in anger. Then in an instant a chase began.

"Bang! Roar! Snap! Bang! Roar! Snap!"

Bill and John never realized they could run so fast. And their intelligence helped them to outwit the dumb reptile.

"I think that beast is called Tyrannosaurus," Bill said. "And he is dumber and slower than Ducky."

"Speaking of Ducky-Ducky," said John. "Look over there. There he is; he's as good as new!"

"Hey," said Bill, "do you think Ducky-Ducky could give us a ride home?"

"What do you think I have been training him for?"

As Bill climbed up on the dinosaur's back he had to admit he'd been wrong. "Yep, maybe Ducky isn't so bad after all!"

Write On #52
UNTOUCHABLE NOUNS

Objectives

1. *Identify nouns*
2. *Create letter scripts*
3. *Introduce Write on #53*

DIRECTIONS

1. Think of some "untouchable nouns." Those are nouns that you cannot see or touch. To help you tell if a word is a noun, put "the" in front of it.

For example:
The fear – yes
The happy – no
The happiness – yes

2. Make a poster page of untouchable nouns that describe feelings.

Emotions are nouns that you cannot touch. You can develop a script which expresses that emotion.

FUN

Boldness

Goofiness

ANGER!!

Match your nouns with adjectives listed in Write On #1.
For example:
The wiggly fun
The red anger
The rising boldness

Write On #53
AN EMOTIONAL POEM

Objective
Writing Poetry

DIRECTIONS

1. Choose one of the words you wrote for Write On # 52.

2. Collect phrases to describe that feeling. What kinds of things might make a person feel that way?

3. Use your word collection to write a poem.

4. Write the title of the poem in the script that expresses that feeling.

Poetry expresses emotions.

A glob of glook, a goop of gluck
A squishy ish or a bunch of bluck,
A bloody nose, a dirty sock,
A bunch of worms under a rock
Yukity, Yukity, Yuck!

Loneliness

Walking to the park alone,
Playing by myself;
No one to share my secrets with,
Whether they're good or bad.
Eating an ice cream cone alone
Loneliness is sad.

Joy

Joy is having a special friend,
Joy is hearing a touching story,
Joy is a warm house on a winter night,
Joy is knowing the King of Glory.

Objectives
1. Report historical events
2. Use first person narrative

DIRECTIONS

1. If you go on a field trip to an historical site, record all the facts that you see or hear. Or use facts from a history lesson or video.

2. Write a journal entry as if you were a real or fictitious person who lived at that time. Use the facts that you have recorded.

A slice of life gives a short glimpse of someone else's life. This writer wrote about the underground railroad after visiting John Brown's cave under the Mayhew's cabin in Nebraska.

On the Underground Railroad

My family and I were slaves from a plantation in the South. A man named John Brown came to our plantation. He did not like slavery. He tried to set slaves free on the underground railroad.

I asked my father, "What is the underground railroad?"

"Well," said my father, "underground means illegal. It is a trail for slaves to go from shelter to shelter. The people who live in the homes hide the slaves from their masters. There are no real trains on the underground railroad."

John Brown told my father, "Go to the Mayhew's cabin in Nebraska City. It is the cabin with three oak trees in front."

My family had to travel there through the dark trees at night so nobody could see us. At least we reached the cabin.

Mrs. Mayhew served us cornbread and dried fruit. I played with the Mayhew's six sons. I was so surprised that so many children lived in one little cabin.

We spent the night in a cave under their cabin. It was dark and spooky down there.

Early in the morning Mr. Mayhew hid us in a wagon. He covered us all up with hay so nobody could find us. After a bumpy, itchy ride the wagon crossed the Missouri River into Iowa to take us to the next underground railroad station.

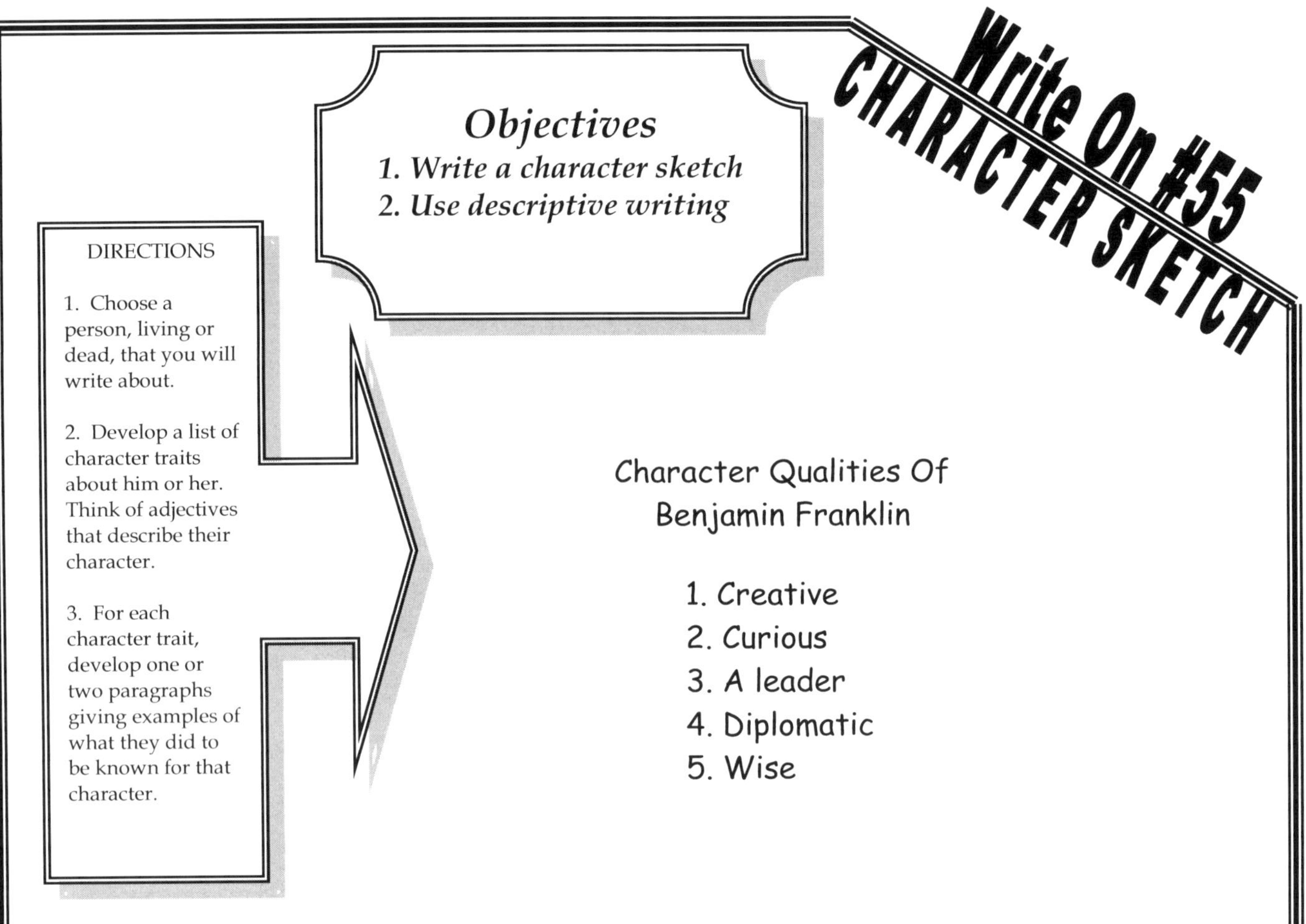

The Character of Ben Franklin

Benjamin Franklin is known for his creative mind and abilities. He was an inventor who invented many things. Among his inventions were a musical instrument, a butter churn, and a calendar.

It was his curious nature that accounted for much of his work. Everyone is familiar with the fact that he flew a kite during a storm to study electricity. Many people for hundreds of years had wondered about lightning, but Benjamin had a curious enough mind that he had to do more than think.

He was also a leader. That is why he came up with so many "firsts" in America. He started the first post office, the first insurance company, and the first fire department. The first university in America was started by him and is still present today. He also helped to start the first hospital. Since these are organizations that cannot be done by one person alone, he had to be a great leader to get other people to make these ideas happen.

Franklin was diplomatic. That is why the colonies sent him to France as a diplomat. The best example of his diplomacy was the Great Compromise. He helped the large states and small states come to an important agreement in developing the Constitution.

All of these things indicate that he was also a wise man. He wrote proverbs such as, "A penny saved is a penny earned." During the Constitutional Convention, he encouraged the delegates to pause for prayer rather than continue arguing over their own states' interests. Perhaps it was his wisdom that guided him to use his other qualities to the good of the whole nation.

Write On #56
SARCASM

Objectives

1. Use humor appropriately
2. Introduce Write On #57

DIRECTIONS

1. Make a list of nouns. Think of adjectives that describe the nouns. Then write an adjective that is the opposite.

2. Or you may think of the adjective first. What is a noun that does not fit that adjective?

Sarcasm should not be cruel. It may be okay to say your dog is as graceful as an avalanche; but it is not okay to say that about your sister. Words can hurt; they should not be used as weapons.

It's about as HAIRY as a PING PONG BALL.

It's about as CLEAN as a PIG PEN.

It's almost as LARGE as a FLEA.

It's just about as PRETTY as a DEAD FISH.

It's about as HOT as an ICICLE.

It's as much FUN as MEASLES.

Scripture has some sarcasm:
A beautiful woman without modesty is like a fine gold ring in a pig's snout. Proverbs 11:22

Objectives

1. *Story writing*
2. *Develop surprise endings*

DIRECTIONS

Write a story using some expressions with sarcasm. Have an unexpected twist at the end of the story.

Mildred's Party

Today was my cousin Mildred's birthday party. Now Mildred is as about as friendly as a snapping turtle, and every bit as polite. So you can imagine my enthusiasm when my Mom said I had to go to her party. I was looking forward to it like a shot in the arm.

My mother also took me to the toy store and insisted I buy Mildred a present. I found a cool box of spiders that would have made a great gift. Unfortunately, my mother took them away and made me buy her a teddy bear in a pink dress: about as useful as a car with three wheels.

We went to the party a little early and found her house as quiet and peaceful as usual – somewhat like a circus. Birthday records and birthday songs and birthday whistles blaring; all to remind us that today was her birthday, as if we might somehow forget. I will admit Mildred looked fairly nice, particularly after she fell in the cake. But she was as spoiled as ever. She needs more toys like a bird needs more feathers.

All in all it wasn't a bad party, although I would have rather stayed home and played baseball. I told Mom I hope I don't have to go to her two-year old birthday party next year.

You may want to try one of these topics:
Going camping with your grandmother
Cooking your first meal
A talent show of 4 and 5 year olds
Your first swimming class

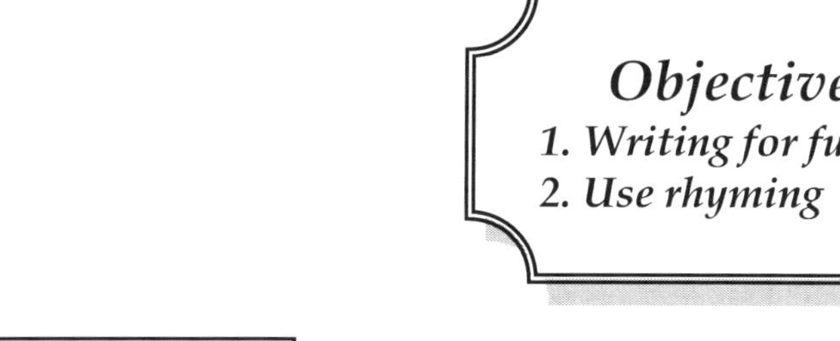

DIRECTIONS

Try writing some epitaphs of your own.

Epitaphs are short, funny rhymes on tombstones.

Under this tomb lies Johnny Brown
The craziest man that ever lived in our town.

Twas a sad, sad day when Miss Julie did sicken
'Cause I can't find her recipe for Southern fried chicken.

Under this stone lies dear Cinderella,
Overdosed on chocolate and vanilla.

Beneath this ground lies Tom on his back,
Was trampled under foot in a hippo attack.

Good ol' Bob lived life to the prime,
He did pretty good to reach one hundred and nine.

Try these starters:
Here in this grave lies Mr. Jones
We are all very sad to see Betty go
Mrs. Smith was the fairest dame in town
Jim Tellabeck lies under this stone

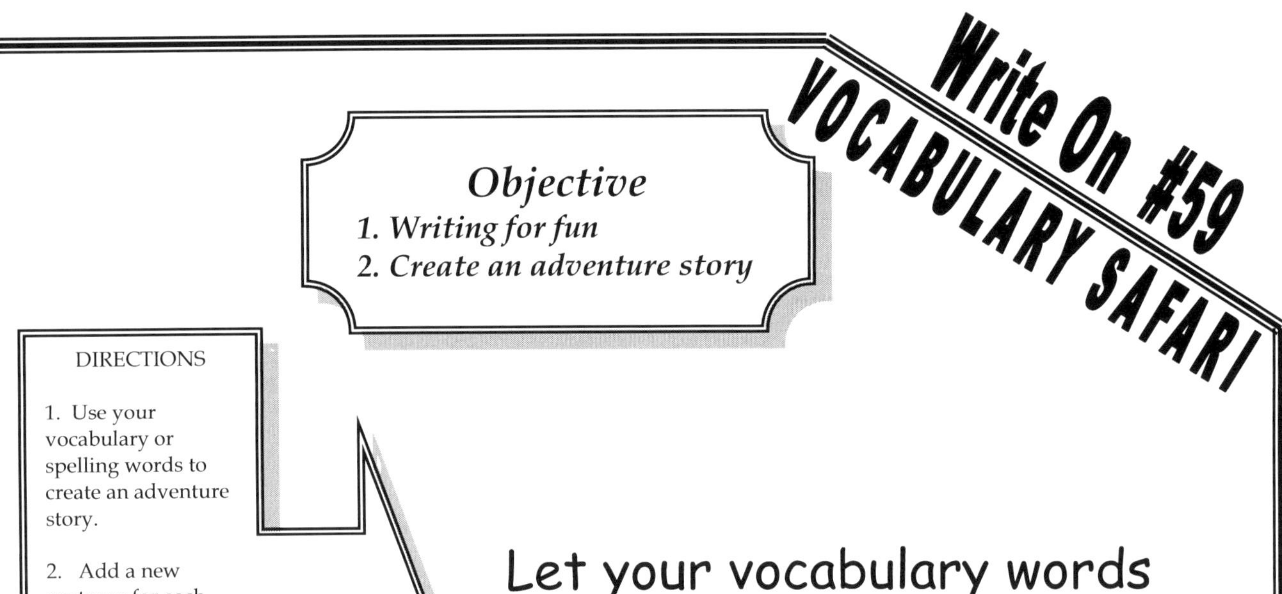

DIRECTIONS

1. Use your vocabulary or spelling words to create an adventure story.

2. Add a new sentence for each word. Let the plot develop with each new sentence.

3. Use your words in the order they appear in your list. Does it take you to unexpected places?

Let your vocabulary words take you on a jungle safari!

On the 29th of February, I started on a safari with my guide to become **oriented** to the ways of the jungle. Unfortunately, we encountered a **cataclysmic** flood. My guide became **melancholy** for fear that the flood would prevent us from crossing. In **retrospect,** it probably would have been better for us to bring a boat along for the crossing.

Since we had no **financiers** to provide money for the boat, we had to make one ourselves. Our emotions were **intrepid** about cutting down trees swarming with insects and snakes. It was also **monotonous** work cutting off branch after branch to make our canoe.

Once we got our canoe in the river, we discovered we had some **logistical** problems, because we wanted to go upstream but the canoe would only go downstream. We felt **invincible** at first, but soon we learned we were not.

We decided to go ashore, but found ourselves in the **chaos** of swarming bees in thick bushes we could not walk through. We had to **congratulate** ourselves when we got through the bees and bushes.

We began again to walk toward our **original** goal upstream. Unfortunately the trail was as **fickle** as the canoe and we got lost. We found some **trinkets** that told us we were near a village. I had to **stifle** my guide's yell. We did not want to seem too **haughty** because we had made our way through the jungle.

Write On #60
A LOOK AT TIME

Objectives
1. Explore timelines
2. Introduce Write On # 61

DIRECTIONS

1. Look at several time lines. How do they list events?

2. On a paper list:
   Centuries
   Decades
   Years
   Months
   Days
   Hours
   Moments

3. For each, think of two examples of events that could be described by that measurement of time.

A timeline is like a map. It can show a large amount of time with little detail, or it can focus on a smaller period and show the finer details.

Time	**Example**
Centuries	Old Testament Prophets
Decades	Exploring the New World
Years	Inventions around 1900
Months	Plymouth Plantation
Days	Battle of Gettysburg
Hours	Paul Revere's Ride
Moments	Explosion of the Space Shuttle

Write On #61 TIMELINE

Objective

1. *Organize material*
2. *Create a timeline*
3. *Introduce Write On #62*

DIRECTIONS

1. Choose one of your topics from Write On #60, or one of the topics below to develop a time line.

2. Use a reference to help you list things in correct order.

Chronology is the order things happen.
Make a chronological time line.

Battle of Gettysburg

July 1, 1863

Battle Began
Northern army pulled back

July 2, 1863

Southern army took the offensive
Confederates attacked the north and south flanks of the Union army but could not drive them out.

July 3, 1863

Southern defeat
Pickett's Charge across open field attacked the center of the Union army but was repelled.

July 4, 1863

Southern troops retreat

Historical Events

The life of a relative

Life cycles of plants or animals

Current events

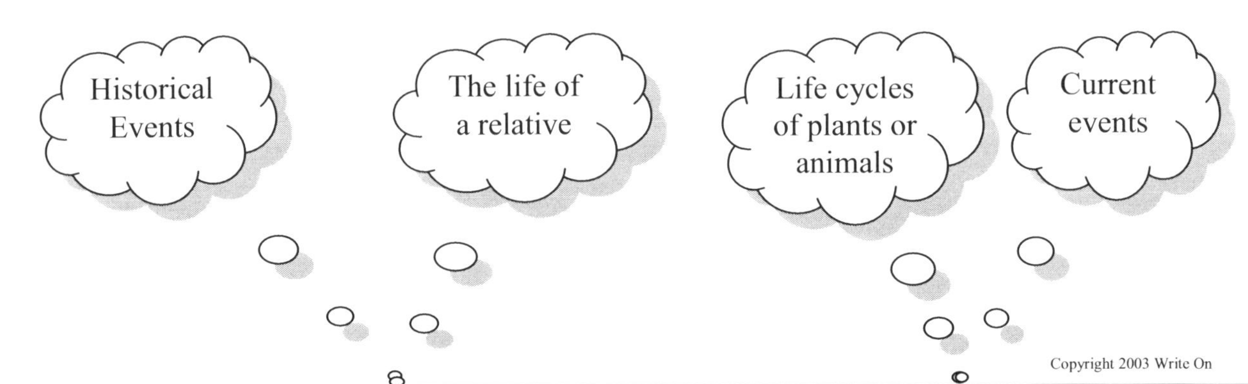

Write On #62
CHRONOLOGICAL ESSAY

Objectives

1. Use a timeline as an outline
2. Write a chronological essay

DIRECTIONS

1. Use the outline from Write On #61. For each point on the outline, develop a topic sentence.

2. Develop a paragraph for each point. Notice that topic sentences do not always have to be the first sentence in the paragraph.

3. Write an introduction and conclusion.

Some essays are arranged chronologically.

Four Days at Gettysburg

In July of 1863 Confederate and Union armies met in the village of Gettysburg, Pennsylvania. For several days the hillsides of that little town became the site of America's bloodiest battleground. The cannons, rifles and yells of wounded men shattered the quiet of the farms and fields in what was to become the beginning of the end of the Civil War.

The battle of Gettysburg began on July 1, 1863. It was by accident that the two armies met there and were engaged in battle at 8:00 in the morning. After more than seven hours of fighting, the Union soldiers fled to their camp. General Robert E. Lee, the Southern commander, had hopes for another victory in battle.

And so the second day of the battle began with hopes for a Southern victory. On July 2 the Confederate army took a definite offensive against the Union troops. Early in the morning the armies lined up along opposing slopes with an open field between them. At four in the afternoon General Lee ordered his troops to attack the Union army at Little Round Top, which was a hill at the southern end of their line. Since the Union army was able to hold Little Round Top at the south, the Confederates then attacked them from the north. Culp's Hill was the northern portion of the Union's line, and by nightfall the Confederate army had taken control of the bottom of this hill. They ceased fighting when it became dark, hoping that with daybreak they would be able to finish taking that northern hill.

At 4:00 A.M. the next morning the armies resumed fighting for control of Culp's Hill. By 11:00 A.M., still unable to drive the Union forces off the hill, General Lee decided to take a different offensive strategy. The men began a cannon brigade firing at the center of the Union line, hoping to weaken them before sending his men on a direct assault. At 3:30 Pickett's Charge began with 12,000 Confederate men charging across an open field in the face of Union artillery. Half the Confederate troops did not make it, and in fifty minutes the fighting ceased with one third of the soldiers on both sides dead or wounded. The Battle of Gettysburg ended on July 3, 1863 with a Confederate defeat.

(Continued on the back)

It was a sad Confederate army that began the retreat on July 4. Wagons carrying wounded men were stretched for miles in a line that headed towards Virginia. The Union army, also weakened by the battle and not wanting to renew the fighting, followed at a distance.

The spirits of the previously undefeated Confederate army were crushed by the outcome of that three day battle. Other battles still remained to be fought. Yet the defeat of the Confederate army had begun at Gettysburg, and a badly wounded nation had a long journey towards recovery ahead.

Write On #63
TONGUE TWISTERS

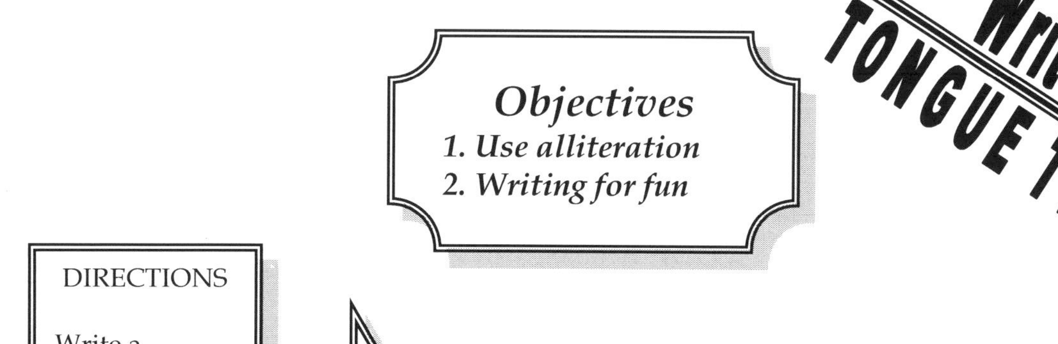

Two twins tested ten tongue twisters!

Betsy's best bugs bite bitter bones.

She shouted "Shazzam!"

Greg grows great grazing grass.

Choo-choos choose chewy chutes.

These sounds can make interesting tongue twisters:
Consonant blends (st, bl, tr, etc.)
Diagraphs (sh, ch, th, wh)

Write On #64
SET YOUR MOOD

Objective
Reflect mood in your writing

DIRECTIONS

1. Choose an activity that you or someone else might do.

2. What mood do you wish to convey?

3. List the steps in order to complete the task.

4. Write at least one paragraph. Each step should have one or more sentences.

5. Each sentence should include words that reflect the mood.

6. To make your sentences more interesting, use variety in choosing the subject of the sentences. Notice the different subjects in the sample writing.

7. Include a topic sentence and a closing sentence.

Even though the writer's mood is disgruntled, he never uses that word. How can the reader tell he is disgruntled?

Mood: Disgruntled

Task: Cleaning my room

Steps: Put away clothes
Put away toys
Make my bed
Empty the trash

I knew my day was getting off to a bad start when my grandmother came in and made me clean my room. First of all, my clothes had to be sorted. So I had to hang up the clean ones and carry the dirty ones all the way to the laundry room. Then she made me put all my toys, which had been conveniently placed where I could use them, back into the closet, completely out of the way. Even the trash can, which was only three-quarters full, had to be emptied. Finally, the last indignity was suffered when she insisted my bed be made. Doesn't a grandmother understand that the bed will be unmade and the room a mess again by tonight?

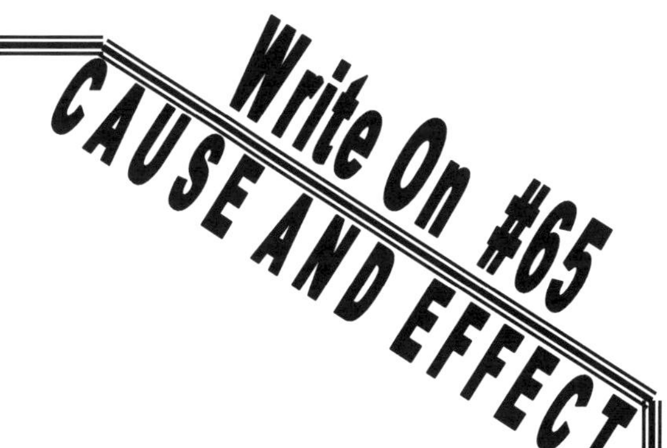

1. *Outline information*
2. *Introduce Write On #66*

DIRECTIONS

1. In this Write On you are going to explain the effects caused by a particular event, person, idea, or object. First you need to choose your topic.

2. Brainstorm the different effects that are caused by your topic. Make a list.

3. Turn your list into an outline.

Cause: Something that makes something else happen.

Effect: The things that are changed.

Here the cause is the invention of cars.
The writer listed three effects.

How cars have changed America

I. Travel further to jobs and schools
II. More recreation
III. Jobs to keep cars going

You might want to consider one of these for a topic:

Effects of an historical event

The effect of a scientific phenomenon

Effect of a person's behavior

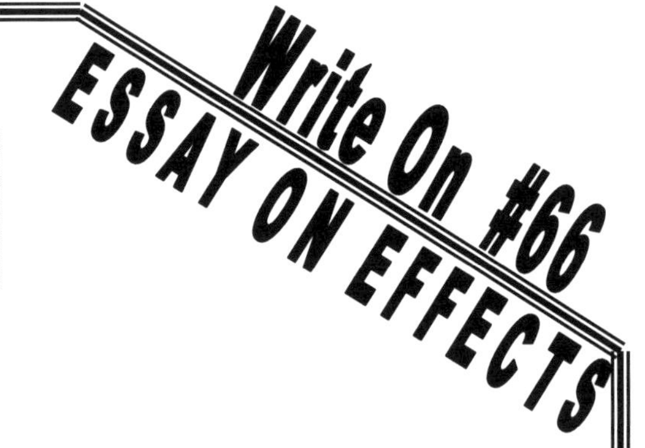

Objectives

1. Develop essay
2. Include topic sentence for entire essay
3. Vary the placement of topic sentences

DIRECTIONS

Use the outline from Write On #62.

1. Your introduction should include a sentence that tells what the essay is about.

1. For each point of your outline, develop a topic sentence.

2. Develop one paragraph for each point. Experiment by placing the topic sentence in different places within the paragraph.

3. Write an introduction and conclusion.

4. Don't forget to give your essay a title.

The introduction includes a topic sentence for the entire essay.

Cars are Driving Americans to Work

Have you ever compared our lives to the lives of the pioneers? Our jobs, schools, and communities are different. **Many of these differences in our lives are due to the existence of cars**.

<u>Because cars take people long distances in a short period of time, people can work miles from their homes.</u> Some people live in one town and work in another. In a single family, people may have jobs or schools miles apart in different directions from their homes. This allows each person more opportunities for jobs or education than anyone imagined 100 years ago.

It is more than just our jobs that are affected. <u>Cars have also expanded our recreation opportunities.</u> If a person lives in a city, there are hundreds of places to drive to within a half hour's drive. Even in most rural areas there are restaurants, stores, and parks in easy driving distance. For those who want to travel a few hours from home, there are numerous vacation spots. For many Americans both skiing and surfing are within a half day's drive. Think of all the additional jobs created by these places of recreation.

Cars do more than just take us to work and play. <u>Automobiles have created many additional occupations simply to keep our cars on the road.</u> Besides the obvious jobs of making and selling autos, other industries have sprung up. The oil industry employs thousands of people. Insurance companies and government agencies have developed. Auto mechanics exist in every town and village.

Yes, with the development of cars the pioneer frontier is gone forever. But cars have given us a new frontier: jobs, schools, and recreation opportunities by the hundreds that are only a drive away. And with a frontier like this, who needs a three month trip in a covered wagon?

Objective
Write math story problems

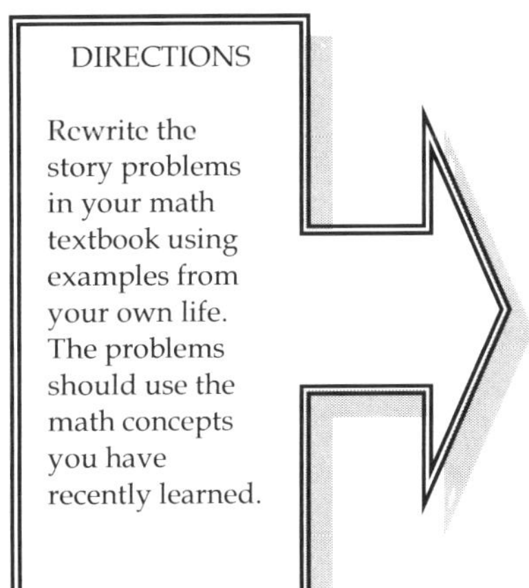

You may understand math story problems better if you write some yourself.

My sister is two years younger than I am. My brother is three years younger than my sister. My mother has made 35 birthday cakes for her kids. How old am I?

Your car holds 25 gallons of gas and gets 22 gallons to the mile. If you drive to and from work on one tank of gas in three and a half days, how far is it from your house to work.

With our new board game, each player gets five $1 bills, five $5 bills and three $10 bills. If there are two players, how much money does the banker have to give out?

I bought a new coat for 25% of the original price. If I paid $26, what was the original price of the coat?

Better yet, make a math test for your favorite aunt and mail it to her.

Make a math test for a younger sibling.

Objectives
1. *Write poetry*
2. *Experiment with prefixes & suffixes*

DIRECTIONS

1. Write a list of common prefixes. Attach some of the prefixes to verbs to make words that aren't in regular use.

2. Attach suffixes to other words to change the part of speech.

3. Only two words in these stanzas need to rhyme.

Prefixes and suffixes make an uncommon poem.

PREFIXATED

You can't unsmile a smile,
You can't unwish a wish.
You can't unpickle a pickle,
And you can't undish a dish.

I've never been dishelpified
Or discoordinated;
I've never been dismessified
Or disfrustrated.

It's never time to resleep,
And never time to redie.
And you never will reeat,
And most certainly won't refly.

Some catalogs list creative descriptions of their products.

Play Ground Sets

PG-251 End summer boredom with this swing set. Two swings, a two seat glider, and 5 foot slide will keep your kids moving. $99.00

PG-252 Imaginative minds will love this play set. It includes a fort, plus two swings, glider for two, and slide. $129.00

PG-253 All you will need is lemonade, because this play set has everything else to keep them happy on summer days. A fort and monkey bars are added to the three swings, two-seat glider, and slide. $149.00

PG-254 Be ready for your kids' friends; this play set will make your back yard the place to be. Two swings, monkey bars, fort, four seat glider, and two seat glider will keep the fun coming all summer long. $179.00

PG-255 Here's our best buy, and the best bet for a summer filled with fun. It comes with three swings plus monkey bars and a four seat glider. Children can slide down the 5 foot slide on one end, or speed through the eight foot spiral slide off of the fort. A perfect playland! $199.00

If you would not be forgotten as soon as you are dead, either write things worth reading or do things worth writing.

Benjamin Franklin

Think like a writer and write like a thinker!

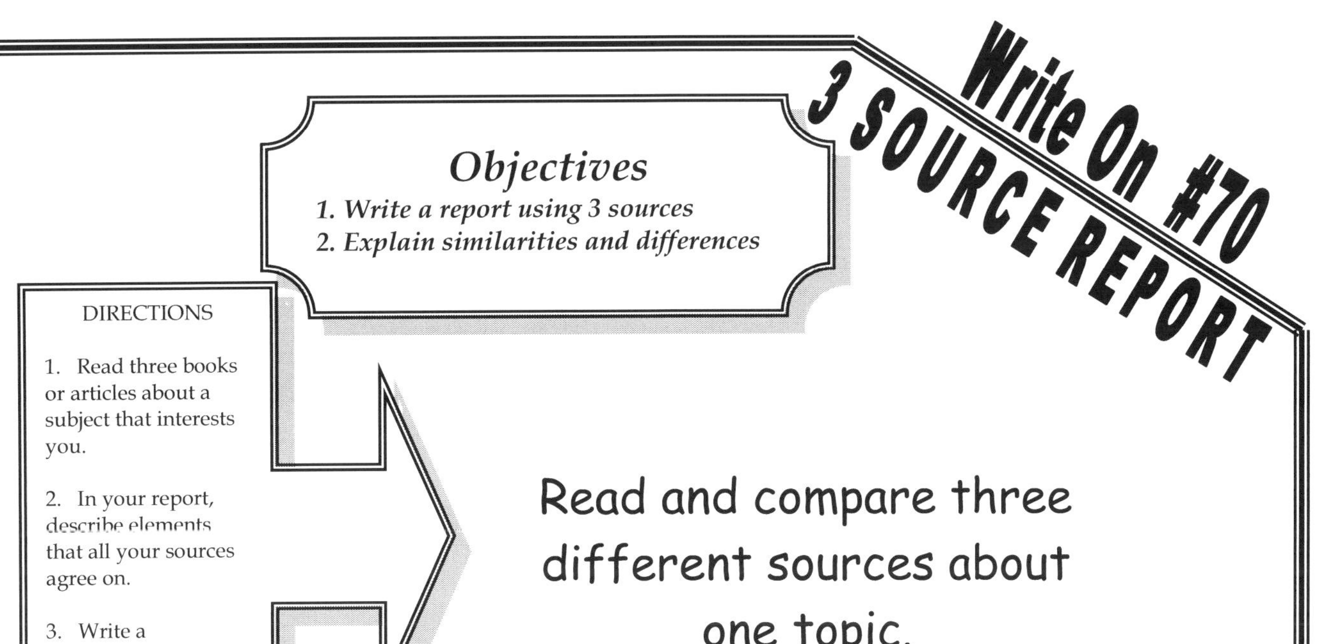

Read and compare three different sources about one topic.

The Mary Celeste

The unsolved case of the *Mary Celeste* is one of the most intriguing mysteries. It is about an abandoned ship that was found afloat at sea. The crew was never heard from.

Many writers have told the story of this ship. The Mary Celeste: an Unsolved Mystery from History by Jane Yolen looks at different theories of what happened to the crew. Kim Dyer who wrote Life in Dark Water also lists numerous theories that have sprouted over the years to attempt to explain the strange occurrence. And new theories continue to arise, such as The Mary Celeste: a Classic Seaquake by Captain D. Williams.

All the writers seem to agree on some basic facts. The ship was sailed by Captain Briggs, who was accompanied by his wife and two year old daughter, and a crew of eight sailors. It left New York on November 15, 1872 carrying 1700 barrels of alcohol to Europe. For the next ten days, the ship's log indicates the ship was on course and experiencing no significant difficulties. The last entry on the log was written November 24.

Obviously, the ship encountered some unknown difficulty after that last entry was written, because on December 4 the ship was found by the crew of the *Dei Cratia* completely abandoned. They searched the *Mary Celeste* and found no one on board.

The ship was in good shape, except that there was a significant amount of water on board. The forward hatch was left open. The chronometer, sextant, register, and navigation book were missing off the ship, though the log was there. The compass was broken and the galley stove was moved. All of the 1700 barrels of alcohol were on board, though 9 barrels were empty. The life boat was also gone. There was no sign of a struggle.

While there may be agreement on the facts described above, there is little agreement as to what may have happened. Jane Yolen presents six of the many different theories of the ship's fate. Many think the ship was attacked by pirates, though there was no evidence of a struggle. Some believe the crew became drunk and killed the captain and his family, though the alcohol on board was not drinkable. Nor does that theory tell what happened to the crew once they took over the ship. So others theorized that the crew became frightened and abandoned the ship, though there is no good evidence for anything frightening to have occurred on board. Thus others have speculated that bad weather caused the crew to leave the ship, though it might be wondered why a crew would leave an intact ship to go out on a smaller life boat. And then there is the conspiracy theory that states that the two captains had developed a scheme in order to get money for the ship. One would wonder why Captain Briggs would have involved his two year old daughter in such a plot.

Kim Dyer lists other improbable theories that surfaced over the years. Sea monsters have been blamed. Fumes from the alcohol might have made the crew fear an explosion. Perhaps the ship was stuck on a moving sandbar, and only become unstuck after the crew abandoned her. From sharks to insurance claims, numerous hypotheses surfaced in the decades after the ship was found.

But the fact that the mystery is over a hundred years old does not prevent new theories from being postulated. Captain D. Williams is convinced that a seaquake, or underwater earthquake, caused the crew to abandon the ship. He points out that the Azores, where the ship was at when the last entry was recorded, is an area with numerous seaquakes. He reports the area experiences at least one seaquake a year. The month after the *Mary Celeste* was abandoned a large seaquake with a magnitude of 8.5 occurred in the area. Is it not possible that smaller seaquakes would have occurred weeks before the larger? The accounts from ships that have experienced a seaquake are quite frightening and could explain why the crew abandoned the ship. It could also explain why the galley stove was moved and the compass was broken.

Perhaps William's theory can explain some of the basic facts regarding the condition of the ship when it was found. But perhaps even those basic facts should be questioned. Some have said that Captain Morehouse, the captain of the *Dei Gratia* who claimed to have found the abandoned ship, was not telling the truth. They doubt the ship could have sailed the distance he claims she did from the time the last entry was written in the log until the day he states he found her floating abandoned. Was Captain Morehouse lying? Is it a coincidence that he had dinner with Captain Briggs the night before Briggs sailed from New York, and then just happened to find her abandoned on the other side of the Atlantic?

And so the theories continue. Perhaps one day a bottle will be found on a deserted island. And inside the bottle there will be a message written by Captain Briggs that will tell us once and for all what happened to him and the rest of those on board the *Mary Celeste*. But unless such an unlikely message, written over 130 years ago should appear, we will probably never know for sure what happened.

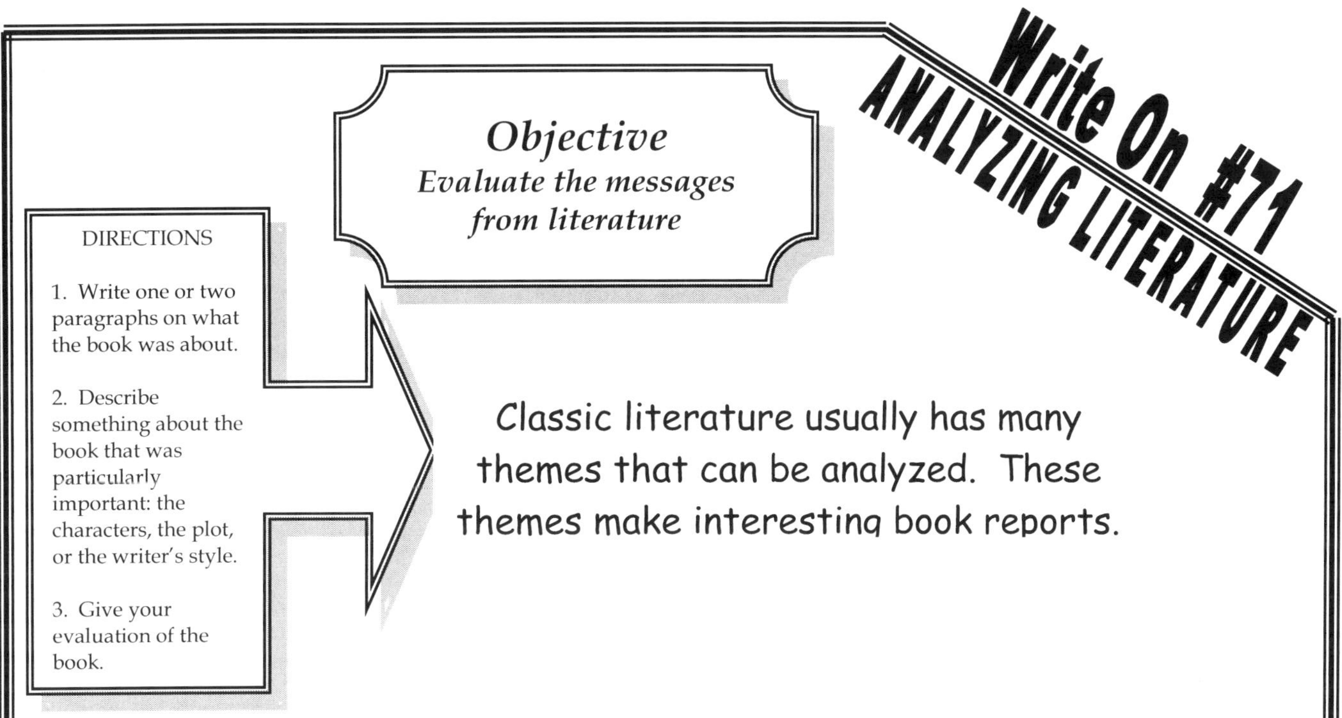

THE BRONZE BOW

The Bronze Bow by Elizabeth Speare is historical fiction that takes place in Galilee at the time of Jesus. The main character is a fictitious boy named Daniel. Daniel is an outcast whose father was killed by the Romans and whose life is filled with hatred and a desire for vengeance. Daniel is part of an outlaw band that lives in the mountains with a plan to raise an army to overthrow the Roman power over Israel. However, things do not turn out for Daniel the way he anticipates; especially after he meets Jesus.

There are a number of significant contrasts in characters through the book. For instance, Daniel is the complete opposite of his new friend, Joel. Joel is a scholar and the son of a wealthy rabbi. Daniel is an orphaned peasant living with an outlaw band. Joel's family is meticulous about observing every detail of the Jewish Law. For the last five years, Daniel has not even known what day the Sabbath was. But the two are bound by their vow to rid the land of the Romans.

The sisters of the two boys are also a contrast. Joel's twin sister, Malthrace, is his friend and shares his adventures. She is lively, vibrant, and unafraid. On the other hand Daniel's sister, Leah, is timid and withdrawn. Since her father's crucifixion she has shut herself up in her house and refuses to come out. Malthrace's offer of friendship helps Leah, but Daniel's hatred of the Romans accidentally destroys Leah's new trust.

The most striking contrast is the difference between Rosh, the leader of the band that Daniel belongs to, and the new teacher, Jesus. Both speak of a new kingdom, but they have very different ideas about what that kingdom should be. Rosh justifies his lifestyle of thieving and attacking caravans, even of his own countrymen, by saying he intends to eventually rid the country of the Romans. Jesus does not attack but speaks of love even to one's enemies. Daniel rejects Jesus' offer to follow him, because he will not give up his hate.

Only when his hate and bitterness have cost him everything, is there hope that Daniel will see the truth about hate and love. But is it too late?

The Bronze Bow is a powerful story of love and hate. It is also a story of adventure, danger, and friendship. It is enjoyable to read and has an unexpected ending.

Write On #72
LYRICS

Objective
Write lyrics

DIRECTIONS

1. The first, second and fifth line of a lyric rhyme. It may help to find two words that rhyme *(i.e. shoe & glue)*

2. Find a name that rhymes with the two words. *(i.e. Sue)* It will be used in the first line. *(My aunt had a donkey named Sue)*

3. The third and fourth lines are shorter and rhyme with each other. They have only five syllables.

Count the number of syllables in each line of a lyric.

There once was a tiger named Ruth
Who always lived in a booth.
She'd call her friend
Who lived at the end
But he never told the truth.

I once knew a lady named Fred
Who ate pickles and cheese with her bread.
Then she'd sit down for tea
With a horse by her knee
And put cream cheese all over his head.

Here are some possible starters:
There once was a bullfrog named
We once had a horse that was red
Some nights when I look at the moon

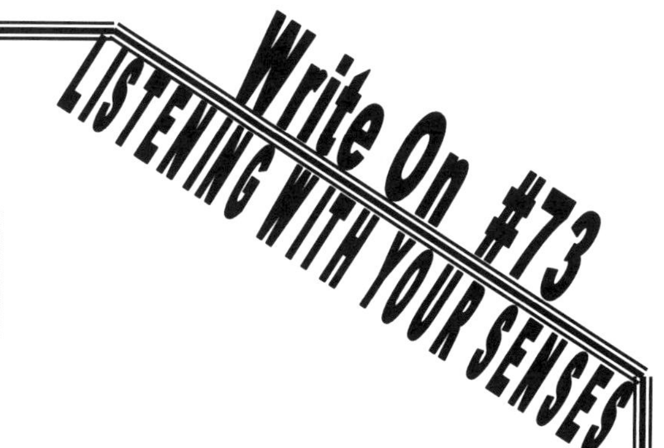

Objectives
1. Write poetry
2. Use senses

DIRECTIONS

1. Choose a subject to write about. Imagine what the people would be thinking. Make a list of all their different thoughts.

2. What would they hear? List the different sounds.

3. Identify all the things they might see with their eyes.

4. What sensations might they touch?

5. Would there be any tastes or smells?

6. After developing your list of all the sensations above, choose the phrases that best describe this experience.

7. Arrange these phrases to form a poem.

Here is a poem describing the fears of the sailors aboard the ships that sailed with Christopher Columbus. The writer tried to imagine what the sailors were seeing, hearing and feeling.

Sea of Darkness

The sea is so dark,
The sea is so scary.
It is as black as night
And dark like death.
The big waves appear,
The sea monster will appear.
Can the ship make it?

Objective
Write a variety of introductions to a story

DIRECTIONS

1. Can you come up with an introduction to a story without using "once upon a time?"

2. Think of a different fable. Write a variety of introductions.

How many ways could the same story start?

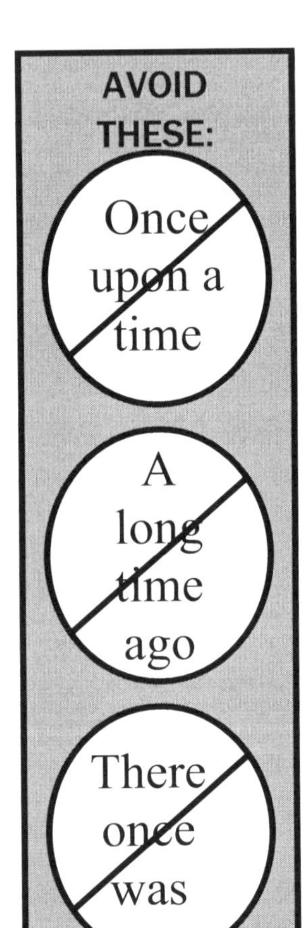

Little Red Riding Hood

Perhaps you have never met Little Red Riding Hood or even been to the great forest that was her home.

It happened so long ago that some people have actually begun to wonder if such a girl as Little Red Riding Hood really ever lived in the great forest.

Little Red Riding Hood – such an unusual name. But it is not nearly as unusual as the adventures she had in this very forest a century ago.

Have you ever walked deep, deep into a forest by yourself, and heard a wild beast creeping up on you? Ask Little Red Riding Hood and she can tell you all about how it happened to her.

People often ask me about the wolf rug hanging on my wall. It belonged to my great-grandfather, who was a respected hunter in these woods many years ago. You see, it all started with a girl, a cute little girl, named Little Red Riding Hood who lived on the other side of the forest.

Objective
Develop topical outlines

DIRECTIONS

1. Choose a topic. List 3 to 5 main sections for that topic. Use Roman Numerals to list the main sections.

2. Develop 2 to 5 points under each main section. Use capital letters.

3. Develop a total of ten different topic outlines. You may consult other books and encyclopedias on ideas of how to organize the outlines.

Organize facts into a topic outline.
Use Roman numerals and letters.

Japan

I. The People
- A. Family Structure
- B. Religions

II. The Land
- A. Geography
- B. Climate
- C. The Ocean

III. The Government
- A. Prior to World War II
- B. Constitution
- C. Prime Minister
- D. Elections

Teeth

I. Facts About Teeth
- A. Primary Teeth
- B. Permanent Teeth
- C. Four Kinds of Teeth

II. How to Keep Your Teeth Healthy
- A. Brush and Floss
- B Eat the Right Foods
- C. See the Dentist

III. Uncared for Teeth
- A. Cavities
- B. Abscess
- C. Peridontal Disease
- D. Missing Teeth

Cocker Spaniel Puppies

I. What is a Cocker Spaniel?
- A. History
- B. Size
- C. Personality

II. Training Your Cocker Spaniel Puppy
- A. Paper Training
- B. How to stop biting and chewing

III. Caring for Your New Pet
- A. Finding a bed
- B. Feeding
- C. Brushing and Cleaning
- D. Playing

Objective
Experiment with onomatopoeia

DIRECTIONS

Think of words whose sound is similar to its meaning.

Onomatopoeia: Words that sound like the sound of the word

Buzzzzz went the bee.

Clippity clop; clippity clop.

Hummmmmm

Drip. Drip. Drip.

Write a descriptive story of someone walking outside or in another setting. Use your list of words.

Tape yourself reading the story. Make the sounds as you say them.

Objective
Develop an annotated bibliography

DIRECTIONS

Write each type of annotation below for one of your favorite books.

An annotated bibliography gives a brief review of the book. Below are different annotations for The Lion, the Witch and the Wardrobe by C.S. Lewis. Macmillan Publishing Company, NY. 1950

Summary Description	This is the story of four British children who disappear into the magical word of Narnia through a closet. They are involved in a delightful, although dangerous, adventure of trying to free the land of Narnia from the control of a wicked witch.
Adjectives	Imaginative, adventurous, magical and fun. Lewis has used a creative way to illustrate some of life's most serious issues.
Who would want to read this book?	Have you ever wanted to visit another world? Do you like adventure and mystery? Young and old, readers will enjoy Lewis' allegory, The Lion, the Witch, and the Wardrobe.
What YOU thought; good and bad.	Lewis has written an enjoyable and delightful story. I wish he had used an animal, however, rather than a witch to illustrate Satan. More pictures in the book would also have been nice.
Tell the real meaning	Aslan, the Great Lion King, sacrifices himself to the White Witch in order to save the captive. This is the story of Christ's triumph over Satan.
Use suspense to make others want to read it	The children journey to the Stone Table to meet Aslan and try to save the land of Narnia and their captured brother from the White Witch. But can they make it to the Stone Table in time before SHE catches THEM?

For a unit study report, make an annotated bibliography of the sources used. Use whichever type of annotation seems most appropriate for that book.

Which type of book would be most appropriate for each annotation listed above?

Objective
Poetry development

DIRECTIONS

1. Look at a tree. Notice its size, shape, and characteristics.

2. Write five words to describe different qualities about it.

3. Write a line describing each word – but don't use the word.

4. Put the lines you have written in any order to form your poem.

Notice the five descriptive words are not in the poems.

The original five words were
tall, strong, green, animals live in it, and shady.

THE OAK

Reaching to the sky,
Mighty are its branches.
The color of life,
Offering shade and shelter to Earth's creatures;
Come beneath my boughs and dream.

The original five words were
busy, falling icicles, graceful, robust, dense

Alive
Growing all over
Falling down in gentle streams
Curtseying, bowing down
In royal splendor
Full of life from deep within
Richly robed in
green

Objectives

1. Write a diametribe
2. Use parts of speech

DIRECTIONS

Line 1 and 7
Two opposite words

Line 2
Two words to describe line 1

Line 3
3 participles (words ending with "ing") to describe Line 2

Line 4a
Two past tense verbs to describe the first part of the poem

Line 4b
Two past tense verbs to describe the last part of the poem

Line 5
3 participles – the opposite of Line 3

Line 6
2 nouns – opposite of Line 2

A diametribe is a diamond shaped poem that uses different parts of speech to move from one word to its opposite.

ON
Lights Sound
Talking Turning Hearing
Listened Watched Played Finished
Ignoring Leaving Stopping
Darkness Silence
OFF

DEATH
The Cross The Grave
Suffering Bleeding Dying
Entombed Descended Ascended Released
Releasing Healing Touching
The Garden The Crowds
ALIVE

Proofread carefully to see if you any words out.

Unknown Author

The wastebasket is the writer's best friend.

Isaac Bashevis Singer

Think like a writer and write like a thinker!

Write On #80
DETAILED OUTLINE

Objective
Develop a detailed outline

DIRECTIONS

1. Look at the outline below. Each digit (1,2,3) represents one paragraph.

2. Using the format of Roman Numerals, Capital Letters, and Digits, write the outline from three articles written by others. These can be textbook chapters, encyclopedia articles or other sources.

3. Develop your own detailed outline

Compare this outline with Write On #75.
The amount of detail has increased.

TEETH

I. Facts About Your Teeth
- A. Primary Teeth
  - 1. 20 baby teeth
  - 2. Infants and children
  - 3. Guide permanent teeth
  - 4. Provide shape to the face
- B. Permanent Teeth
  - 1. 32 Permanent Teeth
  - 2. 6 – 12 years of age
  - 3. Form beneath primary teeth
- C. Four Kinds of Teeth
  - 1. Incisor
  - 2. Cuspid
  - 3. Bicuspid
  - 4. Molar

II. How to Keep Your Teeth Healthy
- A. Brush and Floss
  - 1. Brush after each meal
  - 2. Brush each tooth individually
  - 3. Choosing the right toothbrush
  - 4. How to floss
  - 5. Floss daily
- B. Eat the Right Foods
  - 1. Effect of sugar on enamel
  - 2. Dairy foods strengthen teeth
  - 3. Choices for healthy snacks
- C. See the Dentist
  - 1. High power cleaning to remove plaque
  - 2. X-rays
  - 3. Filling cavities

III. Uncared for Teeth
- A. Cavities
  - 1. Hole in enamel
  - 2. Caused by plaque
- B. Abscess
  - 1. In the pulp cavity
  - 2. Painful
- C. Periodontal Disease
  - 1. Infections of the gums
  - 2. Gingivitis
  - 3. Periodontitis
- D. Missing Teeth
  - 1. Other teeth shift
  - 2. Changes facial shape

Write On #81
MAP DIRECTIONS

Objective
Write clear directions

DIRECTIONS

1. Write the directions to your house or another place from a particular location.

2. Give step by step directions on what roads to turn onto. Use right/left and North, South, East, West.

3. Additional information and landmarks can be indented beneath..

4 . Make sure you give additional information to help identify your home.

Each road is written on a main line. Additional explanations to get to the next turn are indented beneath.

How to get to our house from Highway 83

Go North on Highway 83
- Go 3 miles past Allen City.
- Go to the 2nd light after the railroad tracks.

Turn right onto Bellview Avenue (East.)
- Go 2 blocks.
- There is a fork in the road by the Burger Barn.
- Stay to the left.
- Turn at the next stop sign after the fork.

Turn left onto 8th Street (North.)
- We are the fifth house on the right side.
- Blue house with evergreen tree in front
- 729 N. 8th St.

Have fun with puns.

Clouds reign!

Woodcutters are bored.

A good butler is home **maid.**

What did the glass jar say?
"I can."

Do you know why my cousin has such a small mother?
She is my ant.

Hang up a sign on a door that says, "Once a Pun a Door." Put all your puns on index cards and tape to the door.

Write On #83
SHAPE OF POEMS TO COME

Objective
Writing poetry

DIRECTIONS

1. Choose a subject that would make a good picture poem.
2. Gather information about your poem.
3. Write your poem. Use shapes, fancy script, and different colors.

A poem can take the shape of its subject.

In 1897 the brilliant light of Thomas Edison lit the night

THE GRASSHOPPER

hopping jumping leaping thumping going up coming down on my way

Galaxies swirling stars millions and millions of stars enormous light years across gargantuan immense galactical suns exploding sprinkles of light shining in the universe twirling arms swinging, flinging gases

A
home
for us to share
for us to live in and to
wake up and sleep in to
cook and to eat in, to love
and to laugh and some
times take a bath.

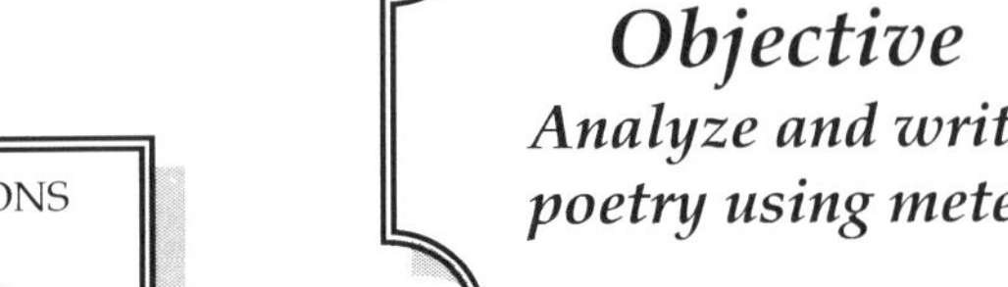

DIRECTIONS

1. Poetry often has rhyme and meter.

2. Choose a poem or song, and count how many syllables are in each line. Old hymns and 18th century poems usually have particularly well developed meter.

3. Choose a totally different subject than the poem or song.

4. Write a poem about your subject, using the same number of syllables per line as the original poem or song.

Rhyming poems have meter. This poem below has a meter of 8,6,8,6. The matching lines rhyme.

Cars

Cars are meant for transportation.
They move from place to place.
They can go throughout the nation.
They go without a trace.

Quitters don't win and winners don't quit.

Elliot Gould

I find that the harder I work, the more luck I seem to have.

Thomas Jefferson

Think like a writer and write like a thinker!

Write On #85
PLANNING PARAGRAPHS

Objective
Plan your paragraph for composition development

DIRECTIONS

1. For each point of your composition you need to plan your paragraphs.

2. Each paragraph should have details that you learn from your research. If you can write the supporting details in the paragraph from facts you already know, there is probably not enough detail.

Compare to Write On #75 and #80. The numbered digits (1,2,3) will become paragraphs. The information under the digits gives supporting details for the paragraphs.

III. Uncared for Teeth
- C. Periodontal Disease
  - 1. Infection of the gums
    - *tissue around teeth*
    - *caused by bacteria*
    - *plaque between teeth and gums*
    - *prevented by brushing*
  - 2. Gingivitis
    - *reversible infection of the gums*
    - *red, swollen, bleeding*
    - *bad breath*
  - 3. Periodontitis
    - *damage to underlying bone structure*
    - *loss of teeth*
    - *may be fatal*

The information written in italics above would usually be handwritten on note cards or paper. Take notes as you read your sources.

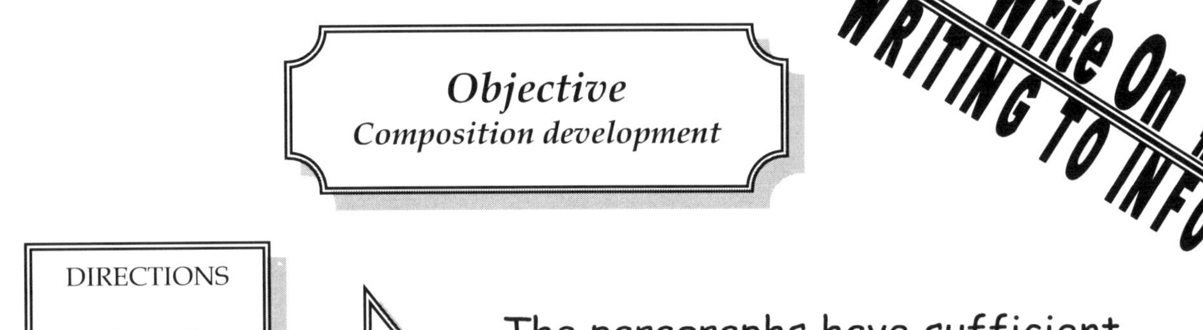

DIRECTIONS

Use the outline from #85 to write one part of your composition.

The paragraphs have sufficient detail that the writer needed to consult a reference.

Periodontal Disease

In addition to cavities and abscesses, lack of dental care can also lead to periodontal disease. Periodontal disease is inflammation of the gums, the pink tissues surrounding the teeth. Plaque accumulates on the teeth and between the teeth. The plaque can seep between the teeth and gum tissue. Then the bacteria in the plaque multiply causing an infection. Periodontal disease can be prevented by brushing teeth.

The first stage of periodontal disease is gingivitis. Gingivitis is a reversible infection of the gum tissues. The gums become bright red and swollen. There may be bleeding, especially after brushing teeth or chewing tough foods. Bad breath often accompanies gingivitis. Once a person gets gingivitis it needs to be treated by a dentist with antibiotics. Otherwise, it may develop into periodontitis.

Periodontitis is a progressive disease that infects the underlying tissues and bones. Once damage is done to the bone structure beneath the gums, the damage cannot be reversed. Periodontitis leads to the loss of teeth. In fact, it is the leading cause of tooth loss in this country, affecting millions of older adults. In some cases it may even be fatal.

Objectives

1. Develop coherence between ideas
2. Introduce Write On #88

DIRECTIONS

1. Is there a topic you would want to convince somebody about? List the reasons for your point of view.

2. Look for coherence. All of your reasons are supporting the same goal.

A writer uses transition words to help the reader make the connection between ideas.

Goal:	People should move to Hempshire Park because it is a great place to live.
Reasons:	
	I. Climate
	II. Beach
	III. Recreation
	IV. Education

Transitional words bring coherence within a paragraph and between paragraphs.

in addition to	similarly	and, but
because of	furthermore	even so
next	in fact	although
then	besides	however
finally	on the contrary	in spite of
therefore	still more	otherwise

T = Transition between points

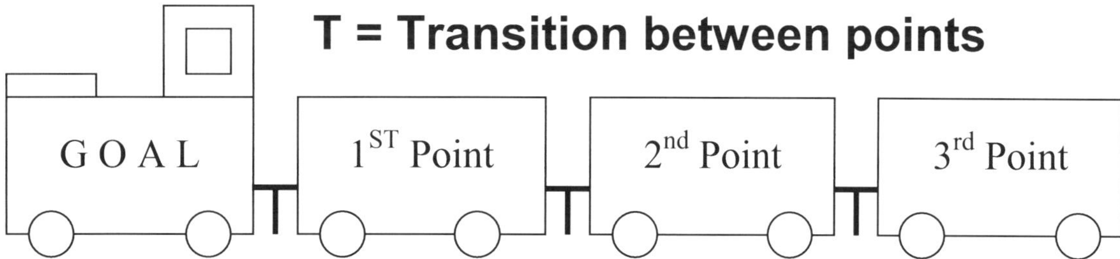

Write On #88
TRANSITIONS

Objectives
Develop transitions between ideas

DIRECTIONS

1. Develop paragraphs to support the reasons listed in Write On #87.

2. Use transitions to show the connection of your ideas.

3. Remember to use an introductory and closing paragraph.

Transition words are bolded.
Read this essay with and without the transition words

Hempshire Park

Hempshire Park is a great place to live. It is a thriving community, perfect for young or old.

First, the warm climate makes Hempshire Park a favorite place. Who wouldn't want to enjoy a delightful summer day without feeling like the sun is roasting you alive. **Or** are you tired of spending the winter digging out of a snowdrift? **Then** consider our mild winters. **Either way**, winter or summer, Hempshire Park's climate is attractive.

In addition to the inviting climate, the beach front development adds character to our town. At the height of the season, tourists flock to the sparkling water. **But even** off season, the shops and restaurants offer the locals all the benefits of a tourist haven.

Plus, Hempshire Park offers our citizens recreational advantages for our citizens that the tourists don't see. **In fact**, the parks and recreational facilities offer every sport kids and adults like to play. **Or** are you interested in concerts, plays, or art museums? There is something for everyone.

Moreover, educational opportunities abound. **Specifically**, there are eight public schools and two private schools for K – 12th grade. **In addition**, there are numerous daycares and nursery schools for the littlest students. **And** for those who have graduated from high school, three colleges and universities are within a half hour drive.

In short, opportunities and a great life are part of our friendly, growing community.

Write On #89
HEART OF A CHARACTER

Objectives
1. Develop a character
2. Write prose

DIRECTIONS

1. Create a character. Write two of three words to describe him or her.

2. Plan a simple task of event that the character might do.

3. Write several paragraphs with your character performing the action. The personality of your character must be reflected in their responses; but do not use the actual descriptive words

The words to describe this character are
heavy, optimistic, playful.
Notice that those words do not show up in the writing.
How can you tell the character's traits?

With the first trace of sunlight, the shrill crow of a rooster broke the quiet of the farm. Mr. Rathers stirred from his sleep. "Ah ha, Mr. Rooster," he chuckled, "so you say I've slept long enough."

With considerable effort, he hoisted his roly poly figure until he was sitting on the edge of his bed. "Hmm, today is Tuesday. Tuesday. Tuesday. What's new about Tuesday?"

Then he remembered. His sister always stopped to pick up supplies every Tuesday.

"Ah yes, Marcy will be here. Wonder what the cantankerous ol' gal will be worked up about today. Well, I'll just make the best of it. No reason not to."

And so Mr. Rathers talked to himself as he got cleaned and shaved, the entire time scheming to devise some mischief to unnerve his older sister this week.

Possible activities for your character to do:

Meet someone on the street
Buy groceries
Find a stray kitten in the yard

Super Bonus:
Have two different characters with different personalities

COMPARE THESE STATEMENTS.

Writing comes more easily if you have something to say.

Sholem Asch

If you're going to be a writer, the first essential is just to write. Do not wait for an idea. Start writing something and the ideas will come.You have to turn the faucet on before the water starts to flow.

Louis L'Amour

Think like a writer and write like a thinker!

Objectives

1. *Gather facts for historical fiction*
2. *Introduce Write On #92*

DIRECTIONS

To write historical fiction, you need to list facts about the time period you are writing about. These facts will be woven into your story.

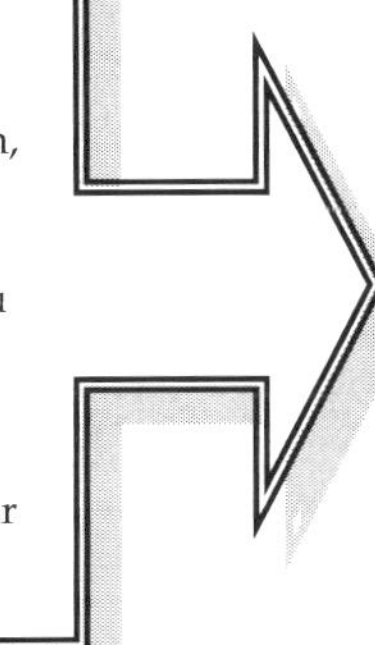

Have you ever noticed how much you can learn about an era by reading historical fiction? That is not an accident but a well planned technique of the author.

FACTS ABOUT THE SETTING: Rome 76 A.D.

Streets are cobbled.

Apian Way

Market place - food sold fresh

Temples to different gods

Caesar claimed to be divine

Roman soldiers dressed in woolen clothes with chain mail

Small mud homes

Christians persecuted

Money had picture of Caesar on it

Merchants were wealthy

Travel by ship around the Mediterranean Sea

Girls often married by age 20

Christians met in catacombs

Slaves from captured lands

Objectives

1. Develop a plot
2. Introduce Write On #92

DIRECTIONS

1. What problem will your main character face? What challenges does he or she face to overcome this problem? What is the final outcome? These can form the chapters of your story.

2. Character development occurs as the character responds to the problems. How is he or she different at the end of the story? Usually the problem the character faces is a universal problem and not just for that time in history.

The story line and character development are planned in advance.

Plot: Apollia tries to escape capture and struggles with bitterness for her parents' deaths.

Characters:
Apollia – 17 year old Christian, parents murdered
Antanna – neighbor who takes her in
Artioch – Roman soldier who murdered her parents for an old family feud. Persecutes Apollia.
Sarai - slave who works in the dungeons
Julia - aunt

Chapter One – Introduction – parents killed
Chapter Two – Funeral
Chapter Three – Captured in market place
Chapter Four – Sarai helps her escape the dungeon
Chapter Five – Travels to another town
Chapter Six – Moves to her aunt's villa
Chapter Seven- Artioch becomes a Christian and apologizes.

Objective

Incorporate character development and historical facts to develop historical fiction.

DIRECTIONS

Write your story from Write On #91. As you do the writing, weave the facts from Write On #90 into your prose. Also reflect the character's personality traits through actions, thoughts, and words.

Historical facts
\+ story line
\+ character development
= historical fiction

This is the first chapter of a seven-chapter story about a Christian girl living in Rome in 76 A.D.

Chapter One

It was a peaceful day in the city of Rome and a seventeen year old girl was taking a walk in the sunshine.

"Oh, I love walking in the sun," thought Apollia while she hummed quietly to herself. "I would love to walk more often, but with my mother being so tired after her long illness it has been impossible to leave her side."

"Apollia, Apollia!" She heard someone calling her name. She turned to see her neighbor, Antanna, running toward her, holding her linen robe up so her sandals would not catch in the fabric.

"Yes, Antanna. What is it?" Is something wrong?"

"Something is very wrong,"said the woman. "About half an hour ago two soldiers came pounding on my door. They asked me if I knew where the house of Marcus was. I did not know what they wanted with your father, so I didn't answer. Then another soldier, I think he was a centurion with the crest on his helmet, came riding up on a horse. They called him Artioch. He pointed to your house and the three started towards your home. I ran to find you."

"Artioch! Oh no, I've got to go!" With that, Apollia ran towards her home.

She ran down the cobbled streets, past the market, past the temple of Zeus, and only slowed down when she got to her house. It was an average Roman house. Made out of plain mud, it had only three rooms, a dining room, kitchen, and bedroom. All members of the family shared the same bedroom. She stopped and looked dreadfully at her home. The door was splintered. She cautiously opened the door then gasped in horror.

Everything that was once in their house was destroyed. Pottery was smashed. Furniture was broken. But where were her parents?

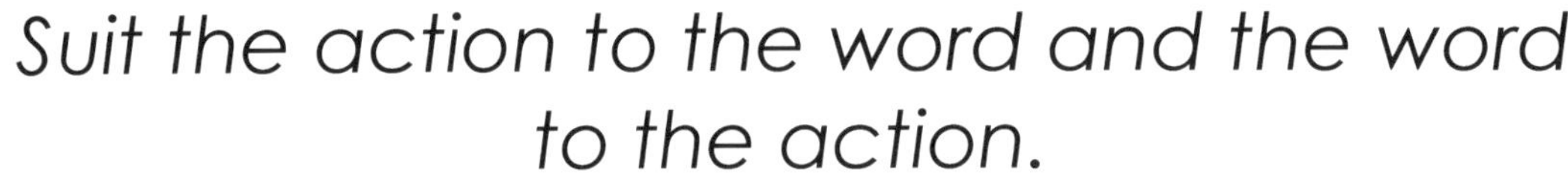

Suit the action to the word and the word to the action.

William Shakespeare

Think like a writer and write like a thinker!

Write On #93
WORDS ARE LIKE...

Objectives
1. Make word pictures
2. Create metaphors

DIRECTIONS

1. Create a word picture with letters that look like the item.

2. Write a metaphor to describe how your picture word compares to written messages.

Picture words can become metaphors.

Words are like CANDY They can be sweet.

Words are like

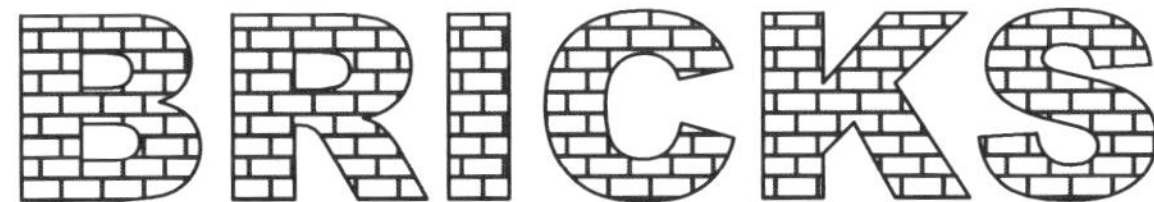

They build sentences.

Write On #94
Let The Scene Be Seen

Objective
Descriptive Writing

DIRECTIONS

1. Describe a scene.

2. Try to capture the sounds, sights, smells , textures and tastes.

3. Include the emotions of the main character.

Try to describe the scene so that the reader experiences it.

Roberta grasped the steaming cup of hot chocolate in her trembling hands. Oh, it was good to get in out of the freezing cold. She pulled the flannel blanket around her tighter as she sipped the sweet beverage and stared towards the fireplace. The crackling blaze was soothing - such a contrast to the howling wind outside.

It was a long walk from his broken car to the only garage station in the next town. The distant lights against the dark sky appeared several miles away. The loudest sound he heard was the crunch of gravel beneath his feet. Crickets chirped, owls hooted, the occasional bark of a dog was heard somewhere to the south. Suddenly, he heard a rasping sound nearby which made his heart stop.

You may have seen nature pictures in the four seasons. Try to write descriptive paragraphs of a particular scene in:

- Different seasons
- Different times of day
- Different emotions

Write On #95
THESIS STATEMENTS

Objective
Write thesis statements

DIRECTIONS

1. Study the thesis statements below.

2. Write a thesis statement for five different subject areas you are studying. (You may include hobbies or areas of special interest.)

3. Look for thesis statements in articles and chapters you read.

A thesis statement:

- is an idea or concept
- is the subject of a composition
- acts like a road map for the composition.

Examples of Thesis Statements

The Civil War changed the relationship between the federal and state governments.

Forest fires disrupt the food chain.

The influence of the Greek system of education can be seen in American schools.

Playing soccer provides valuable skills to the athletes.

Important comparisons exist between the Sermon on the Mount and Paul's Epistle to the Romans.

Mark Twain used humor to explore serious issues.

Proteins are essential to life.

Hint: Many thesis statements show how one thing (or person) has impacted or influenced something else.

Objective

Outline and write a persuasive composition

DIRECTIONS

1. Choose a topic you would like to convince others about.
2. Do your research. Gather facts to support your position.
3. Write your thesis statement.
4. Organize your main reasons into an outline.
5. Write your composition.

Here is an outline for a composition to persuade.
All points support the thesis statement.
Facts are used to convince others.

TOPIC: Infant Nutrition
THESIS: Breastfeeding is the best source of nutrition for infants.
OUTLINE:

I. Health benefits of breast milk for infants
- A. Reduction in colic
- B. Reduction in Sudden Infant Death Syndrome (SIDS)
- C. Healthier Immune System
  - 1. Less allergies
  - 2. Less infections

II. Long-term benefit for individuals who were breastfed as infants
- A. Decreased incidence of certain diseases
  - 1. Less asthma
  - 2. Less Crone's Disease
  - 3. Less incidence of certain cancers
  - 4. Less diabetes
  - 5. Less obesity
- B. Dental development
  - 1. Decreased dental cavities
  - 2. Decreased orthodontics

III. Health benefits to mother
- A. Decreased weight loss at birth
- B. Decreased incidence of breast cancer
- C. Decreased rate of hemorrhage
- D. Decreased postpartum depression

IV. Other benefits to breastfeeding
- A. Convenience
  - 1. no bottles to prepare
  - 2. less dishes
- B. Cost

DIRECTIONS

1. Compare two persons, objects, eras of history, or phenomenon.

2. Make a list of similarities and differences.

3. Write a thesis statement comparing the two.

4. Develop an outline.

Objectives

1. Write a composition
2. Introduce Write On #98

Interesting and thought provoking compositions can be developed from comparisons.

THESIS: Although they were bitter enemies, Hitler and Stalin shared many characteristics as world leaders.

I. CHILDHOOD
- A. Hitler
  - 1. Date of birth — April 20, 1889
  - 2. Education — Did poorly in school
  - 3. Family — Death of 2 siblings and both parents
- B. Stalin
  - 1. Date of birth — December 21, 1891
  - 2. Family — Only child to survive infancy; Death of father
- C. Comparison
  - 1. Era - Old World Politics at turn of century
  - 2. Deaths of father's - Hitler 13 years; Stalin 14 years

II. EARLY POLITICAL ACTIVISM
- A. Hitler
  - 1. Political views — Hatred towards Communist and Jews
  - 2. Declared revolution Nov 8, 1923 – 2000 armed Nazis
  - 3. Arrested and imprisoned for attempted revolution
- B. Stalin
  - 1. Political views — Social Democratic
  - 2. Organized strikes and demonstrations
  - 3. Arrested April 18, 1902
- C. Comparison
  - 1. Sponsored violence
  - 2. Arrested
  - 3. Angry and bitter from imprisonment

III. RISE TO POWER
- A. Hitler
  - 1. Changed from armed encounters to constitutional law
  - 2. Popular speaker
  - 3. Won 32% of votes in 1932
  - 4. Chancellor under Hindenburg
  - 5. Took over Germany after Hindenburg's death in 1934
- B. Stalin
  - 1. Took Lenin's place after his death in 1921
  - 2. Political opposition from Trotsky
- C. Comparison
  - 1. Took power after death of previous leader
  - 2. Use of violence and assassination

V. RACISM AND GENOCIDE
- A. Hitler – 6 million Jews in concentration camps
- B. Stalin – killed more of his own people
- C. Comparison – Both anti-Semitic
  - Hitler killed for hatred/racism – Stalin for political power
  - Both mass murderers
    - but Stalin never held accountable by the rest of the world

IV. WORLD WAR II
- A. Hitler
  - 1. Attacked Poland in 1940
  - 2. Concentration camps for Jews
  - 3. Planned to attack USSR
- B. Stalin
  - 1. Declared War on Germany
  - 2. Invaded Germany and defeated 1000 year Reich
- C. Comparison – Lust for Power

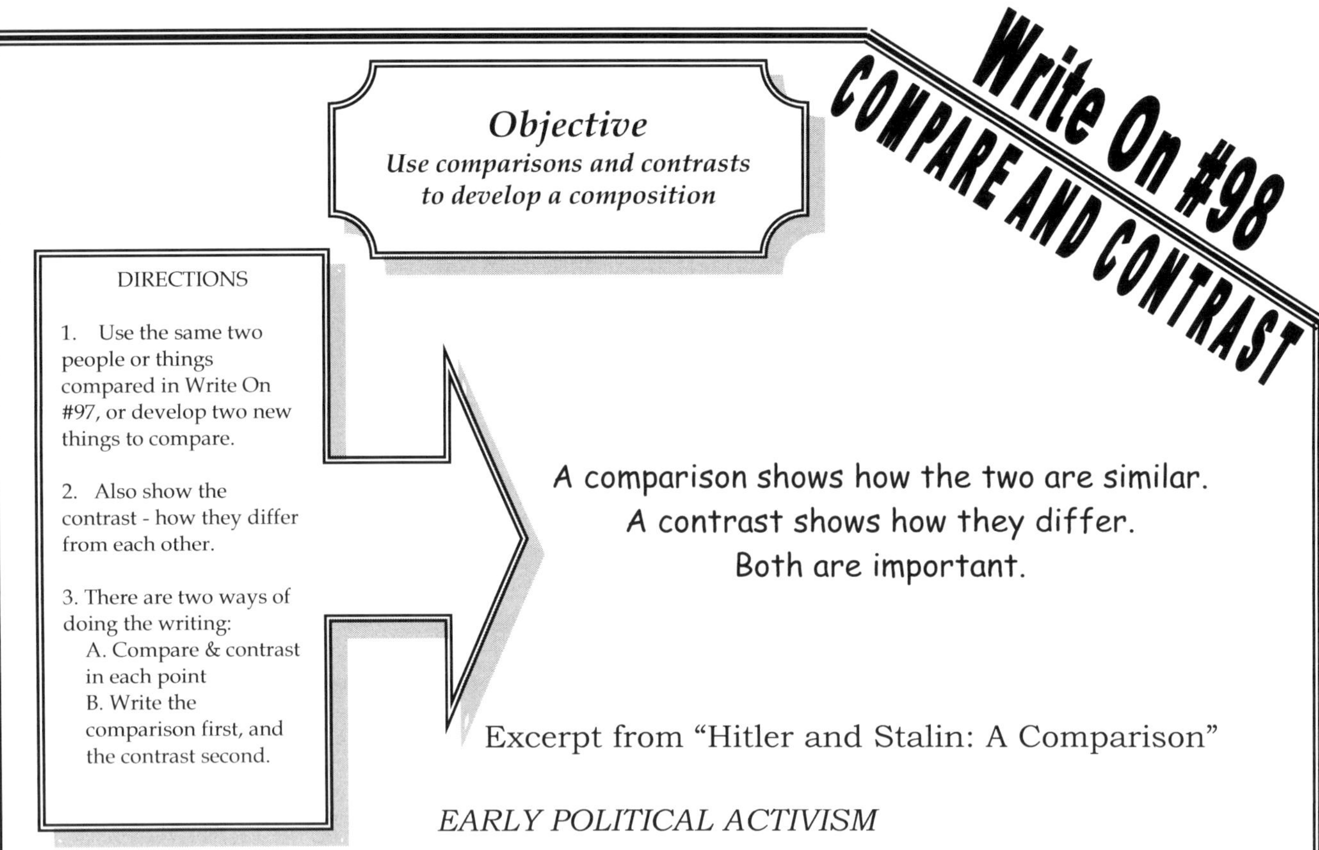

Excerpt from "Hitler and Stalin: A Comparison"

EARLY POLITICAL ACTIVISM

From the beginning of his political life, Hitler was motivated by hate. He hated Communists because of their political views. He hated Jewish people because of their race. There were numerous Communists and Jews in Germany at this time.

On October 30, 1923 Hitler was at a rally and announced he was prepared to march on Berlin and eliminate the capitol city of all Jews and Communists there. Less than two weeks later, on November 8, 1923, he held another rally and declared a revolution. The following day he led 2000 armed Nazis to take over the Bavarian government. This attempt failed and he was arrested.

Stalin's political activism started two decades before Hitler's. Like Hitler, he began by organizing strikes and demonstrations. In 1901 he joined the Social Democratic Party and worked full time in revolutionary work. In both Tiflis and Batum he organized workers in strikes and demonstrations. He was arrested on April 18, 1902 in Batum.

While the two leaders had different political views and belonged to different political parties, similarities between the two exist. Though they declared different groups of people their enemies, they both were militant against their enemies from the beginning. They were both radical idealists, even to the point of killing others to uphold their own ideals. They both accepted and practiced violence for political reasons even before they had any political power themselves, and their tactics were almost the same. Both Hitler and Stalin were arrested for their revolutionary work. And both of them became angrier because of their imprisonment. And the anger of these men, who were not yet recognized leaders, was about to change the world.

Write On #99
WRITING TO DEFEND

Objective

Organize information to defend a position

DIRECTIONS

1. Chose a position where there are opposing views.

2. Read about both sides of the argument.

3. Give reasons for defending one position.

4. Answer the arguments from the other side.

Letters to the editor of a local newspaper often defend a position.

THESIS:
While some people believe safety regulations are unnecessary government regulation, such safety measures have, in fact, saved numerous lives.

OUTLINE:

I. Statistics
- *A. Increase in driving since 1950*
  - *1. 10 times more vehicles in America*
  - *2. 8 times more licensed drivers*
  - *3. People driving further to work and recreation*
- *B. Number of fatalities*
  - *1. No increase in fatalities since 1950*
  - *2. Should be 10 times greater due to increased cars/miles driven*
  - *3. Safety regulations effective*

II. Specific Safety Regulations
- *A. Seat Belts*
  - *1. Keep passengers in car*
  - *2. Prevent bodily impact against hard objects*
  - *3. Fibers designed to break individually to survive the crash*
- *B. Air bags*
  - *1. Decreased fatalities in cars with air bags*
  - *2. Prevent bodily impact*
  - *3. Dangerous for children*
- *C. Child Safety Seats*
  - *1. Protects weak neck and back of infants*
  - *2. Infants unharmed in accidents where all others killed*
  - *3. Teaches young children not to wrestle in car*

III. Myths
- *A. Seat belts are dangerous*
- *B. Safety features are too expensive*

AGREE OR DISAGREE?

The time to begin writing an article is when you have finished it to your satisfaction. By that time, you begin to clearly and logically perceive what it is you really wanted to say?

Mark Twain

Think like a writer and write like a thinker!

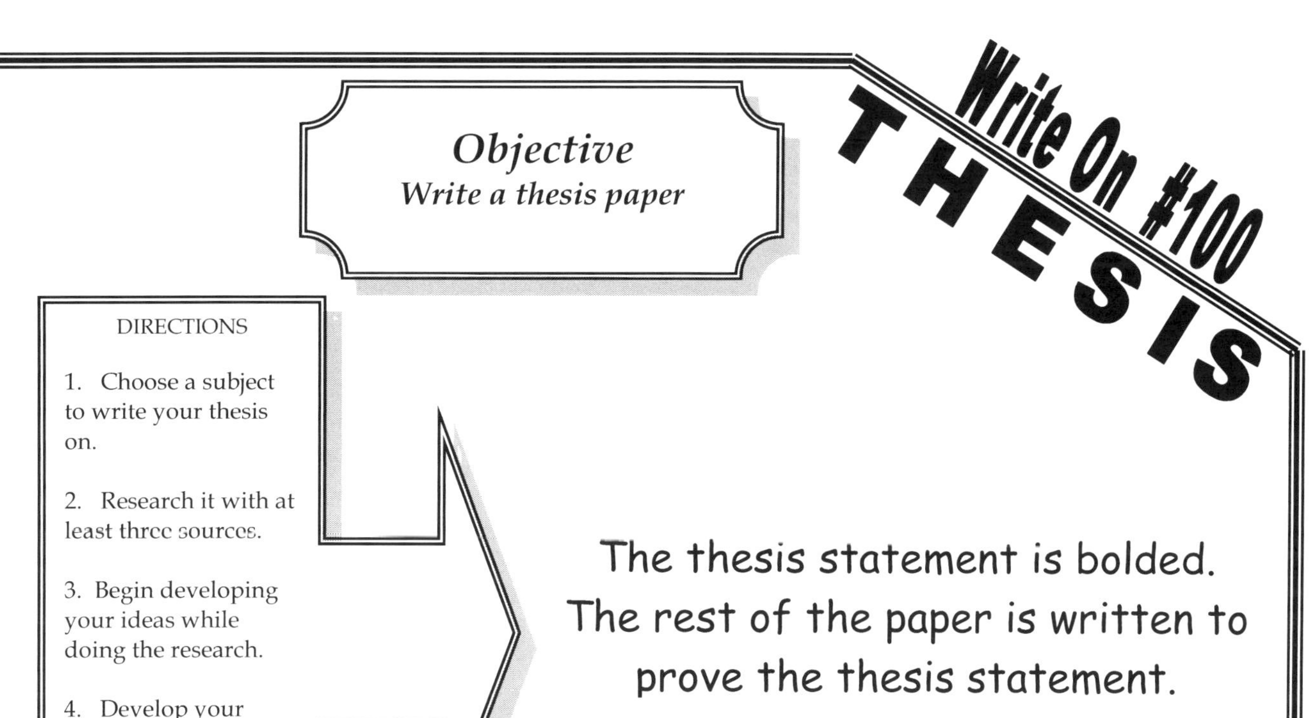

The Making of a Legend

Many generations of English and American youth have enjoyed the legends of Robin Hood and King Arthur. They might be surprised to know that these very British tales were influenced by a French noblewoman, Eleanor of Aquitaine. **The influence of Eleanor of Aquitaine permeates the stories of Robin Hood and King Arthur.**

INTRODUCTION – THE DEVELOPMENT OF A LEGEND

Legends develop over time and cannot be attributed to a single source. In the case of both Robin and Arthur, a variety of written accounts appeared over the years with similarities and differences between the different accounts.

In both cases, a well-published writer collected and edited the stories to create the popular versions that we now know. Sir Thomas Mallory wrote the Arthurian legends in 1485; about one thousand years after some believe the real Arthur may have lived. Howard Pyle wrote the story Robin Hood and His Merry Men. These became the "official" stories in the popular mind, similar to the way the Disney version of Snow White or other tales become commonly known.

There is immense value to these popular versions. First, the authors derived their tales from a number of older sources. Second, they wove together a tale using elements of literary style such as plot, climax, and character development. This gives a form of unity to the various exploits of the characters as well as endearing them to the hearts of English teachers, thus ensuring another generation of readers.

But historians prefer to study the older, less popular versions and to probe even further back into the oral traditions behind them. For our purposes, we are interested in the influence of Eleanor, who lived five hundred years after Arthur may have lived and contemporaneously with the legend of Robin Hood.

WHO WAS ROBIN HOOD?

One cannot read of the exploits of the well-known outlaw without pondering the question of who he really was. Did he, in fact, even exist? It is generally believed that Robin Hood was a real person about whom oral legends developed. Literary historians would love nothing more than to find an autobiography written by this individual, but there is no written material on him until two centuries after his era.

But one can readily find when and where this Robin Hood lived, which does lend credibility to the possibility of his existence. The tales take place during the captivity of King Richard the Lionhearted while his brother John reigned in England in his place. That dates the events between 1192 and 1194 A.D. Also, a modern map of England can be consulted to find the location of Nottingham, a real village. One can even visit Sherwood Forest and imagine the Merry Men lurking in the woods, and debate the old question if robbing the rich to feed the poor is indeed an ethical occupation.

WHO WAS KING ARTHUR?

The attempt to find the date and locale of King Arthur is another matter. Search the lists of the kings of England long and hard, but one will not come across any King Arthur and Queen Guinevere. Nor will one have better success finding Camelot, for no maps, modern or historic, will show it.

But before one dismisses the Arthurian legends as pure fiction because of lack of historical credence, go back a little further in time. Before William the Conqueror led his forces onto English soil in 1066 to become the first King of England, the British Isles were populated and ruled by local lords. These lords bore more similarity to a chieftain than a king, but they did rule over their own lands and peoples. Stonehenge and the accounts of the Romans who attacked the British Isles give evidence of these local groups and their leaders. Could Arthur have been the king of such a group?

To a young person who watches films about Arthur and Robin Hood, it might seem at first that Robin Hood would be the more ancient character. The armor of Arthur was more advanced, as was his code of chivalry. It might seem that Arthur, had he lived, would have lived after Robin Hood and King Richard. Such reasoning would lead one to conclude he did not exist, in that all kings and queens after William the Conqueror have been accounted for; and our legendary Arthur is not among them.

But before dismissing Arthur, notice that some fragments of life in ancient Britain exist in the embellished Arthurian legends. The presence of the magician Merlin points to an early date, in that magic was banned in Europe during the Middle Ages. Also, the knights of King Arthur battle other kingdoms without ever crossing the English Channel. That, too, reflects the domain of local chieftains prior to the unification of England.